INDIA DESIGN YEAR BOOK

02 2014

PENGUIN ENTERPRISE
Published by the Penguin Group
Penguin Books India Pvt. Ltd, 7th Floor, Infinity Tower C, DLF Cyber City, Gurgaon 122 002, Haryana, India
Penguin Group (USA) Inc., 375 Hudson Street, New York, New York 10014, USA
Penguin Group (Canada), 90 Eglinton Avenue East, Suite 700, Toronto, Ontario, M4P 2Y3, Canada
Penguin Books Ltd, 80 Strand, London WC2R 0RL, England
Penguin Ireland, 25 St Stephen's Green, Dublin 2, Ireland (a division of Penguin Books Ltd)
Penguin Group (Australia), 707 Collins Street, Melbourne, Victoria 3008, Australia
Penguin Group (NZ), 67 Apollo Drive, Rosedale, Auckland 0632, New Zealand
Penguin Books (South Africa) (Pty) Ltd, Block D, Rosebank Office Park, 181 Jan Smuts Avenue, Parktown North, Johannesburg 2193, South Africa

Penguin Books Ltd, Registered Offices: 80 Strand, London WC2R 0RL, England

First published in Penguin Enterprise by Penguin Books India 2015
Penguin Enterprise is the custom publishing imprint of Penguin Books India

10 9 8 7 6 5 4 3 2 1

ISBN: 9780670088447

Art direction and design by Lemon Design Pvt. Ltd, Pune
Printed at Replika Press Pvt. Ltd, India

A PENGUIN RANDOM HOUSE COMPANY

CII INDIA DESIGN YEARBOOK 2014

FOREWORD

Make in India: Making It Happen by Design

Design has been the most appreciated yet undervalued asset of our times. Design is everywhere. It is all around us. Design transcends all aspects of our daily lives, be it at work, at home or for leisure. Every time we have a good experience, a good feeling, it is by design. Every time we are dissatisfied, feeling let down, it is a case of inadequate or bad design.

Good design helps to bring about tangible economic and financial dividends in attracting talent and business and fostering creativity. A maturing and growing India requires excellence in design as it is no longer merely desirable but an essential feature of life. Attaining excellence requires attention to be paid not just to high standards in aesthetics and functionality but also to the increasingly important elements of environmental sustainability, social inclusiveness and our heritage.

India has enjoyed a long history of design appreciation, with art, design and craft successfully woven into our culture and all facets of our lives. As we regain our place amongst the world's leading economies, it's time to regain our lost magic.

Another challenge before us is to help policymakers and business professionals appreciate design beyond mere aesthetics and guide them in understanding the importance of integrating design into our enterprises to develop innovation-driven industries, processes and products.

The Make in India mission is a pivotal statement made in recent times about the importance of revitalizing our manufacturing sector. The well-being of our manufacturing industries is an imperative, as it is a source of employment and of innovation. Make in India is not only about attracting Indian and foreign investment but is also concerned with improving the performance and competitiveness of the sector along with a distinct focus on innovation.

All data indicators and forecasts suggest that India's growth is likely to accelerate towards its high potential, and in a manner that is sustainable over the long term. India is witnessing a renewed wave of growth in manufacturing which promises to be much more rewarding than earlier ones.

While there is positivity all around, it is necessary to take a proactive look at how we can strengthen the Make in India mission. Design has a significant role to play in revitalizing the manufacturing sector and in creating new avenues for growth. Design is an essential element of the kind of innovation that is required to improve economic competitiveness. When designers work with companies, they can ignite innovation. Just as a small gear moves the bigger gear, designers transmit creative energy into larger companies.

A key element that will determine the future of manufacturing in India is the private sector's investment in design. Additionally, with the government embracing design in the delivery of public services, its contract with citizens to improve quality of life will be better fulfilled. Globally, it has been demonstrated that companies that use design are more successful than those that don't. Companies using design are more likely to be developing new products and services — and twice as likely to experience sustainable growth.

Design is a word that describes both a process as well as an outcome. As a process, it turns ideas into material things. It is an occupation, which makes the world around us easier and pleasurable. The words Design and Innovation are also interchangeable as both are concerned with the creation of something new that creates social or economic value.

Design is helpful in creating desirable products as also in the integration and application of new technology. It enhances the brand image of an organization and is key to the creation of new markets. As former Sony chairman Norio Ohga put it, 'The product itself must be good, but it must also make the customer think,"I'm glad I bought it," "I'm glad I use it," "I'm glad I have it." Design is an aesthetic interpretation of technology.'

Embracing design-driven innovation can greatly increase manufacturing competitiveness. A strong value-focus will result in high-quality products that can succeed in a competitive global economy. As capital becomes abundant and a business-oriented government supports growth, Indian companies will need to look beyond our borders to transition from being low-cost suppliers of parts to becoming innovative creators of value. Design will be at the centre of this transformation.

Today, there is a sense of self-assuredness amongst design firms in India. Our designers are taking a holistic approach to innovation in optimizing form, function, sustainability and the economic viability of new products. They are providing design solutions and creating innovations that are truly world-class.

The CII India Design Yearbook is a mechanism to communicate the purpose of design beyond just aesthetics. We hope that celebration of the success stories listed here, showcasing design excellence, will inspire young designers as well as emerging businesses, some of which will grow into world leaders.

Udayant Malhoutra

Chairman & Managing Director
Dynamatics Technologies Ltd

Chairman
CII National Committee on Design

MESSAGE

The Government of India, and particularly the Department of Industrial Policy & Promotion (DIPP), recognize the importance of design as a significant economic contributor. We recognize design as a building block of innovation and as an important contributor to realize the Make in India mission.

We realize that design is an important factor to improve everyday life for all sections of Indian society and give the world a sense of our cultural identity — how our history and place have been shaped, and the concept of who we are and how we live.

Design capability is about employing vision, process, creativity and technical skill to develop products, services and brands that capture the imagination of customers throughout the world. The effective use of design requires a better understanding of what it is, what it does and what it can contribute.

Publications such as The CII India Design Yearbook will surely go a long way in improving the understanding of the various roles and benefits of design and hence would encourage organizations to embrace design more and more.

I am very happy to have been invited to be a part of this publication. I would particularly like to congratulate all the designers for their remarkable work, which I very much look forward to reading. I commend CII for conceiving this publication.

Amitabh Kant

Secretary

Department of Industrial Policy & Promotion
Government of India

PREFACE

Welcome to The CII India Design Yearbook 2014.

For the last fifteen years, CII has been performing the role of India's strategic body for promoting and leveraging design towards sustainable economic growth. It has strenuously and diligently worked to demonstrate and promote the vital role of design in making businesses more competitive and public services more effective. The yearbook contained in these pages is yet another one of the landmark CII initiatives to promote design.

The yearbook is a compilation of the best of design work created, produced and launched in the preceding year in India. The design projects presented in this yearbook showcase the richness and range of design in India. It is a reference work, the purpose of which is to present comprehensive and illustrative information about the myriad manifestations of design.

The yearbook also features the winners of the CII Design Excellence Awards 2014. The CII Design Excellence Awards discover the new paradigms of design in India, which answers the call of making Indian industry and manufacturing more competitive and innovative. The awards showcase the emerging face of design in India and its newer manifestations. The awards set the standard for design in India and are the ultimate accolade for good design.

The yearbook was conceived to fill a gap. Until now, there has been no authoritative source which provided — in one place — an account of recent trends in the world of design, the state of the design industry and its successes.

The second edition of the yearbook carries forward the character of the first yearbook as an archive of the best design work. We hope to improve it year by year, and would be glad to receive your suggestions and comments.

In closing, I would like to thank the contributors of this book for their engagement in this publication, the members of the CII National Committee on Design for their support as well as the CII team that has been instrumental in the yearbook's production.

Chandrajit Banerjee

Director General
Confederation of Indian Industry

EDITORIAL BOARD

Members of the CII National Committee on Design

Satish Gokhale
Director
Industrial Design
Design Directions Pvt. Ltd

A graduate of India's premier design institute, National Institute of Design (NID) in Ahmedabad, Satish's firm, Design Directions Pvt. Ltd, founded in 1988 by him and his better half, Falguni — also a graduate of NID Ahmedabad — combines design, technology, aesthetics and relevant materials to create a major impact on industrial, medical, electronic and consumer products. Design Direction's focus is on brand strategy, industrial design, visual communication and user interface design.

Satish is a recipient of several local and international awards. Just to name one, he is the recipient of the Design of the Decade Award, instituted by the Industrial Designers Society of America (IDSA), for a low-cost water filter designed for the Tata Group. He also recently received a Red Dot Award in Germany and a 'G Mark' (Good Design Mark) in Japan for an indigenously designed solar-based computing device — Mobiliz.

Satish has served as jury member on several design award committees — locally and overseas. He is a founder member of the Association of Designers of India (ADI), and is a past member of the India Design Council (IDC). He is also a member of the CII Committee on Design. He is currently the chairman of the design committee at the Mahratta Chamber of Commerce Industries and Agriculture. He has been invited to speak at many national and international design conferences.

Through his work, Satish has been able to raise a great level of awareness towards design in hard-core engineering sectors and prove to them by sheer market success, the importance and benefits of industrial design. He has, till date, successfully designed and launched over 650 products in the Indian and international markets for a host of clients, ranging from the small-scale sector to the heavy-industry sector.

Some of Satish's products are sold in over forty countries. He holds many patents and design registrations, most of which have been licensed.

Hrridaysh Deshpande
Director
DYPDC Center for Automotive
Research and Studies

Hrridaysh has been in the field of education for over twenty-one years. Presently, Hrridaysh is the member of the governing body of Ajeenkya D.Y. Patil University, and is the director of DYPDC School of Design and DYPWWI School of Film and Media.

Additionally, he works as the consultant adviser to India Design Council, a national strategic body of the Government of India, established under the aegis of the Department of Industrial Policy & Promotion. He is the member of the CII National Committee on Design.

Earlier, he founded Creative-i College in 2004, one of India's first private initiatives in the field of design education. He was the director of Multiversity School of Professional Engineering. Here, he designed and executed a unique master's programme in engineering design for graduate engineers.

Hrridaysh is an experienced, enthusiastic, and energetic educator and innovation facilitator. He is passionately committed to education and is capable of expanding the limits of traditional pedagogy through the development and realization of a unique integrative and interdisciplinary curriculum.

EDITORIAL BOARD

Members of the CII National Committee on Design

Anil Sain Mathur
COO — Godrej Interio
Godrej & Boyce Mfg Co. Ltd

Mr Anil Mathur, COO (Chief Operating Officer), Godrej Interio, has been instrumental in diversifying Godrej & Boyce Mfg Co. Ltd from a predominantly office-furniture and home-storage business into home furniture, interiors, laboratory engineering solutions, health care and modular accommodation for ships, to make it a single-window solutions provider for the home as well as workspaces.

He is a member of the CII National Committee on Design, and is the chairman of CII — Furniture & Fittings Skill Council.

He is also one of the founder members and the current president of the Association of Furniture Manufacturers of India (AFMI).

Pankaj Jhunja
General Manager — Design
Tata Motors

Design is my profession by choice, and I have been lucky to have had an opportunity to be associated with this very challenging and satisfying profession for the last twenty-three years of my working life.

This association has seen me mature from creating designs to creating design organizations, from designing simple, low-technology products to highly complex products like the automobile, in various responsibilities as a designer, design manager, project manager, and both purchaser and seller of design services, with companies like Milton Plastics, Thermax Culligan, Dilip Chhabria Design, Renault India and, now, Tata Motors.

Having graduated as a mechanical engineer from NIT Silchar, he did his post-graduation from IDC, IIT Mumbai, in 1991. He has also had a chance to further the cause of design, in a limited way, through his association with design bodies, policymakers, and academic institutes.

Suresh Sethi

Director
Global Consumer Design Asia
& VP — Whirlpool India

Suresh Sethi has built a unique and extensive track record in design, innovation and brand leadership. Suresh is currently the vice president, South Asia, Whirlpool Design, and he works consistently to align creative process with business. China and India have half the world's consumers. As the region becomes the global business hub, designers have a responsibility of shaping this new landscape, where design will blossom from observing the real world, and bring about the flowering of goodness in the lives of millions.

Manjunatha Hebbar

Senior Vice President, and Head of
Product Realization, Cyient Ltd

Manjunatha Hebbar has over twenty-seven years of experience in the global product-engineering and R&D business. Starting as an entrepreneur with a focus on new concept/new product development, he led a design lab for over thirteen years that developed and licensed over eighty-seven original products in avionics, telecom, networking, medical electronics, consumer electronics and industrial automation domains. Later, he played key global engineering and strategic leadership roles at Philips Software Centre, Agere Systems (Proxim — Wireless), iGATE Global Solutions and HCL Technologies. Currently, he heads the Product Realization business unit for Cyient Ltd.

He has been a part of several industry bodies and associations like NASSCOM, IESA, IMA, has engaged in promoting and nurturing strategic alliances and ecosystem development. He is a core member of the CII National Design Council. He is the founder of Swayamprakasha — a self-reliance foundation promoting, supporting and nurturing self-reliance amongst the needy. He is an electronics engineer with MBA in systems and marketing. He also has a fellowship in strategic management, with a focus on business sustainability and social entrepreneurship.

Milind Joshi

Manager, R & D
Forbes Marshall Pvt. Ltd

Mr Milind Joshi is the R & D head of the steam systems division and industrial design at Forbes Marshall Pvt. Ltd. He is responsible for their IPR activities. He is the member of the CII National Committee on Design and has also been involved with CII as the jury from industry for the institute evaluation exercise under AICTE — CII Survey of Best Industry-Linked Technical Institutes. Mr Joshi has five patents in his name. He completed his BE in mechanical engineering from Pune University in 1990. He also completed the Stanford Ignite course, from the Stanford Graduate School of Business, for innovation and entrepreneurship in 2013.

He has a total work experience of twenty-two years, out of which ten years have been in the field of production and tooling. For the past twelve years he has dealt with New Product Ideation and New Product Development. He had worked with Forbes Marshall from 1990–94 also and then moved to Tata Motors. He rejoined Forbes in 2000 and, since then, has worked in its R & D Division.

CONTENTS

INDUSTRIAL DESIGN

INTERACTION DESIGN

MOBILITY DESIGN

VISUAL COMMUNICATION

02 2014

INDUSTRIAL DESIGN

Differniture

Design Firm:
Differniture

Project:
The topographic coffee-table

Design Team:
Aakriti Kumar

PROJECT TITLE

The topographic coffee-table

BACKGROUND

Our focus was to create a furniture piece that would merge sculpture and functionality in a sustainable manner. The target was to use a mundane material that is readily available and transform it into a piece of usable art.

CHALLENGE

The biggest question to answer when creating a product is to address the wastage that occurs during production. The challenge was to look at a sustainable solution to the problem, with an approach of reducing waste.

SOLUTION

We created a zero-waste design for this table. The material that was allotted for this project would be used entirely without discarding anything. Once that was finalized, it was easy to know what material would be best suited for the task. Since we wanted to use an easily accessible material, we went with plywood. Taking inspiration from nature is a great way to understand sculptural forms, thus we studied topography and translated it into our designs. The detailing for the tabletop was created with the use of reclaimed wood that we salvaged to top off our sustainably designed coffee-table.

CLIENT SPEAK

This piece was a great learning experience about using plywood as an external material rather than hiding it behind a veneer and using it for constructing doors/cupboards. We all have preconceived motions about what things should be made of and look like; it was while prototyping that we learnt it is better to challenge the norms, for that is how one creates something unique.

ABOUT THE DESIGN FIRM

Differniture is a young furniture design atelier foundered by Aakriti Kumar, an alumna of the Parsons School for Design, New York. After graduating in the field of product design at the age of twenty four, she conceived Differniture, where she designs and produces alternative, sustainable furniture, with an equal emphasis on form and functionality.

SERVICES

- Creating a zero-waste design strategy
- Using reclaimed and discarded wood as raw material
- Following a cradle-to-cradle approach in production
- Merging a strong sculptural presence with a function in the design process
- Creating innovative forms of furniture by using easily accessible material (plywood) in a unique way
- Giving form and functionality equal importance in the designs
- Nature and naturally occurring phenomenon play an important role in Differniture's collection

420, Sector 42, Gurgaon 122 009, Haryana

Aakriti Kumar

+91 97117 67119

differniture@gmail.com

www.differniture.wordpress.com

PROJECT TITLE

MAC — Master Air Controller

BACKGROUND

This is a compressed air-control system which helps reduce energy consumption by controlling the balance between the demand and supply sides. It helps compressors work for longer without any fluctuations, thus saving the load on it and consequently saving energy.

CHALLENGE

The challenge was to provide a complete package which enables the plant operator to view the functioning of the system along with allowing him to control the valve automatically and accurately, on the basis of the pressure inputs given to the system.

SOLUTION

The MAC directly gives a visual indication, which displays the pressure in the line, set point pressure, control valve position, status of the bypass valve, etc. In addition to this, it gives an alarm indication if the pressure in the line goes above the maximum set limit pressure. As such, the plant operator can view the functioning of this system on one screen. The control valve is operated by the system, automatically and accurately, on the basis of the pressure inputs given to the MAC.

Design Firm:
Forbes Marshall Pvt. Ltd

Project:
MAC — Master Air Controller

Design Team:
Shashank Wanwe, Kunal Ghate

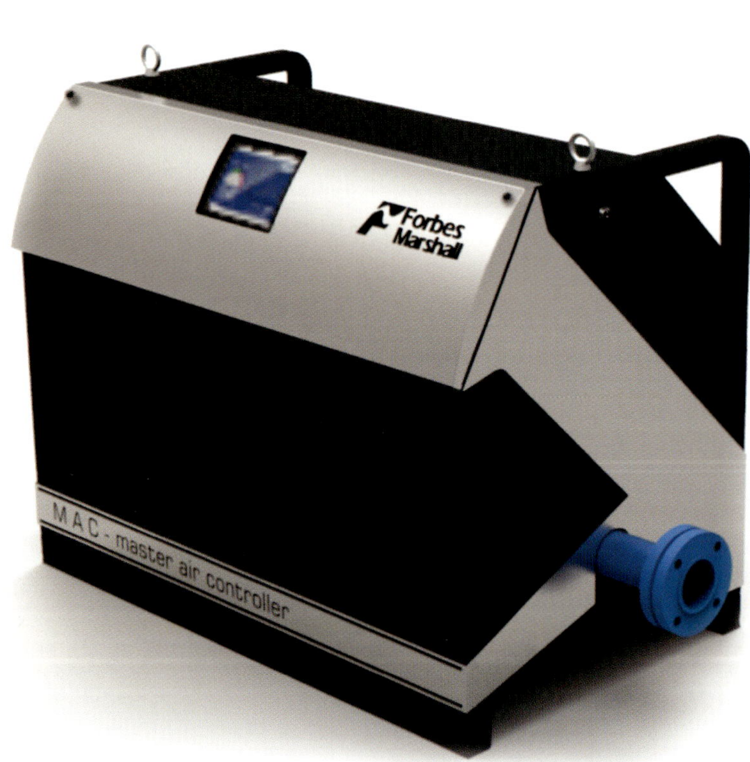

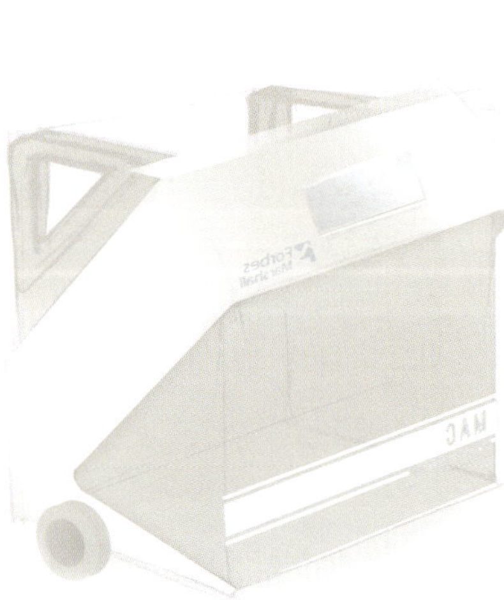

CLIENT SPEAK

MAC provides a user-friendly touch screen display. This display exhibits the real-time status of the system and its parameters. This is an online system that continuously monitors and controls the system parameters and keeps the process variable in its limit values. By navigating through various screens on the panel, one can get a clear picture of the system in operation and thus control becomes easier.

SERVICES

- The LCD is placed at an ergonomic angle, which gives complete screen visibility to the user
- Minimum use of fasteners provides ease of assembly & maintenance, while also making it look less cluttered
- Single-point locking makes it easy to open & close from the sides
- Compact design
- Strong visual aesthetics

A-31, MIDC Estate, H Block, Pimpri, Pune 411 018, Maharashtra

Mr Kunal Ghate

+91 93218 64814, +91 20 3985 1257

kghate@forbesmarshall.com

www.forbesmarshall.com

Man machine interaction

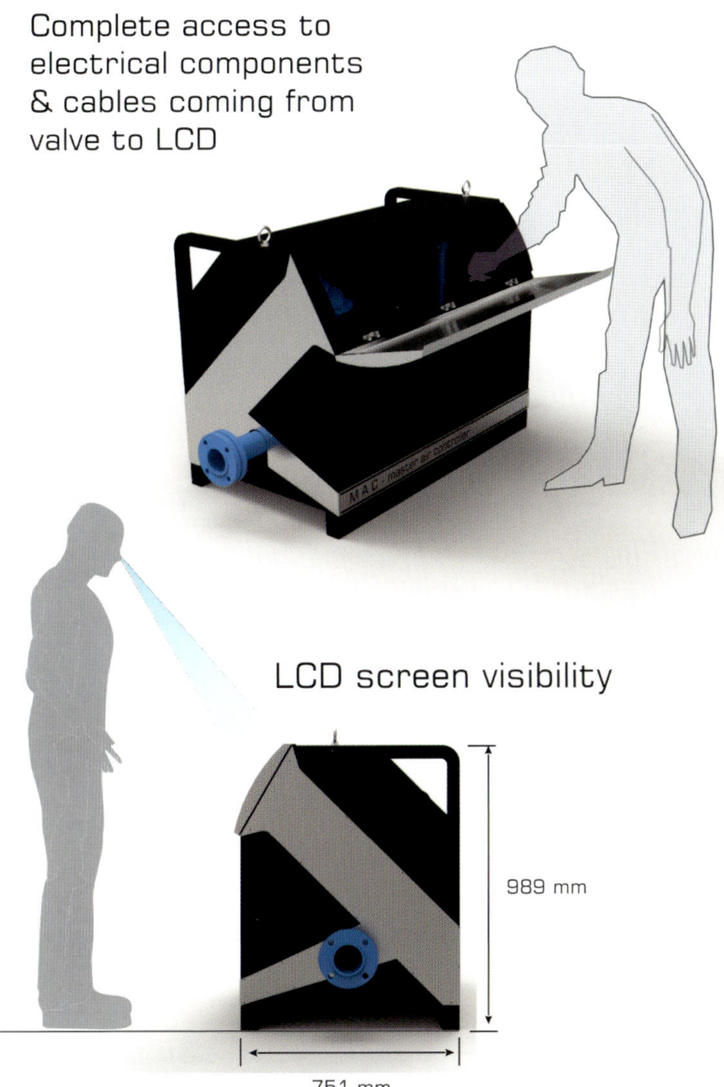

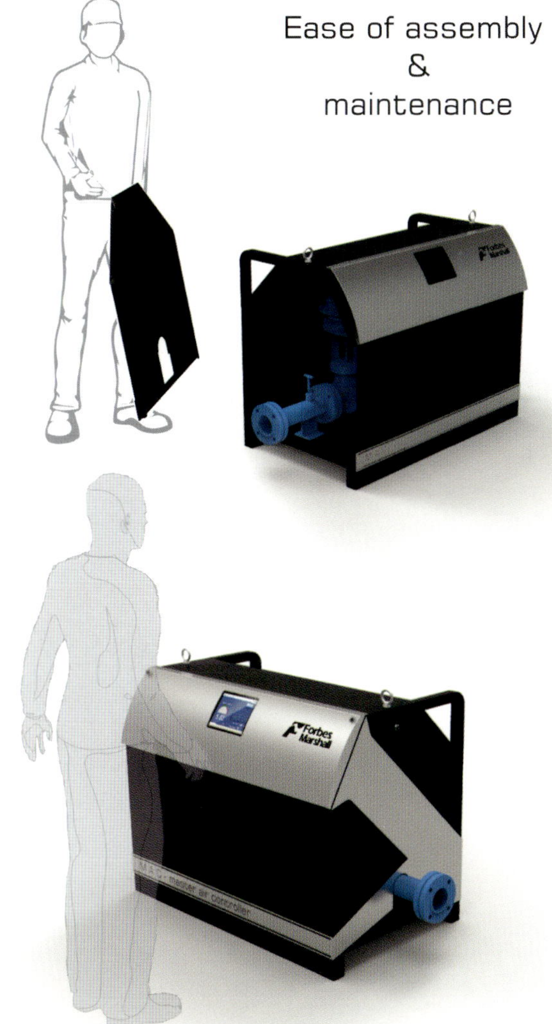

Design Firm:
Furlenco

Project:
Pico — Home Furniture Range

Client:
Furlenco, Bangalore

Design Team:
Naina Shenoy

PROJECT TITLE

Designing furniture for a furniture rental company. The quality of the furniture has to be good, with usage of solid wood.

BACKGROUND

First- ever range designed for the first-ever organized furniture rental company in India, Furlenco. This requires the furniture pieces entering and departing numerous Indian homes, used repeatedly by various kinds of people and, most importantly, catering to a comfortable lifestyle for these various consumers.

CHALLENGE

Designing for a furniture rental company. Making products for easy assembly, warehouse storage as well as ensuring that they are aesthetically pleasing and ergonomically comfortable.

SOLUTION

Urban India includes innumerable kinds of people, with innumerable tastes and preferences. How can we make furniture an enjoyable experience aesthetically as well as ensuring they are functional. Pico's style and form strives to be chosen for varied Furlenco homes. Designer furniture does not mean only custom-made furniture; also, rented furniture does not mean old, faded or jugaad furniture. Pico is made in large quantities so as to allow as many families and re-locators to live comfortably and maintain the lifestyle they are used to. Pico components are designed to help the manufacturing process start and end smoothly, catering to in-time batch productions.

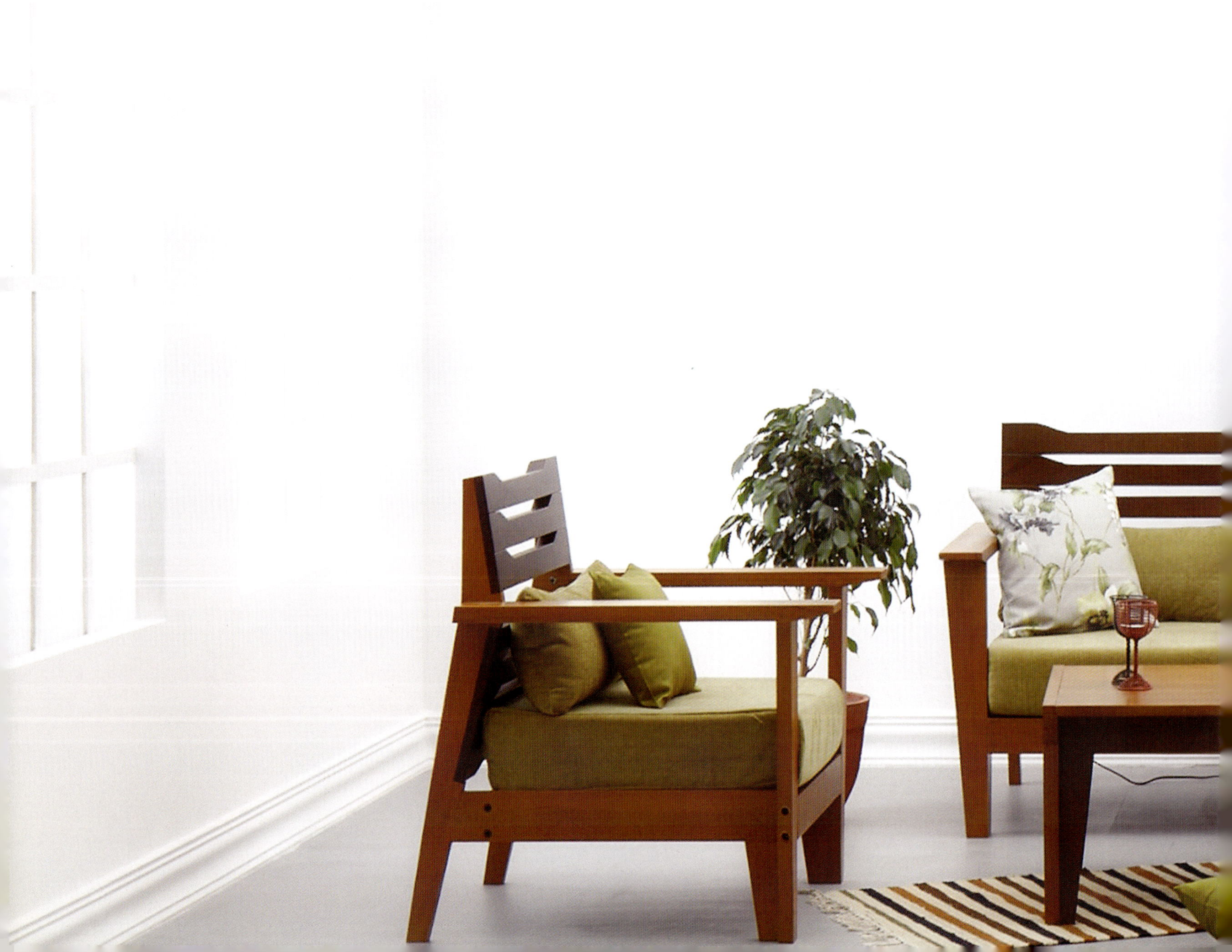

CLIENT SPEAK

Pankaj Baruah (Vice President Operations): 'Pico design embodies a mix of traditional Indian choices with contemporary looks. It has an earthy feel as well as a modern, stylish outlook. It has also been designed so as to make it suitable for mass production. Pico is flat-packed, which makes it easy to handle, and seeing a box convert into a beautiful structure is an amazing experience.'

ABOUT THE DESIGN FIRM

Furlenco — Themed Furniture Experiences, is the first-ever organized home furniture lending company. While it is a lending company, it also believes in creating its own home furniture solutions for its customers. It strives to be an innovative company, with its own in-house design lab. The firm is design-driven and is a constant practitioner of design thinking. We have varied heads (tech, marketing, sales, etc.) along with designers developing product solutions for our customers.

#34, Technopark, 80 Feet Road,
AVS Compound, Koramangala,
Bangalore 560 034, Karnataka

Naina Shenoy

+91 80 8801 1888

design@furlenco.com

www.furlenco.com

Design Firm:
Future Factory

Project:
H2.0

Client:
Harbauer India [P] Ltd

Design Team:
Jashish Kambli, Poorva Lavate, Kunal Borkar, Virang Akhiyaniya and Chintan Ghatalia

PROJECT TITLE

Harbauer 2.0

BACKGROUND

H2.0 brings safe water to local Indian communities. It is designed to bring technologies, used in addressing post-war arsenic contamination in Germany, to local schools in the Indian Ganges delta, where such natural contamination causes serious health hazards.

CHALLENGE

The considerations of bringing water technology of such a large scale to a small local community deals with several issues. Some of these are: (1) an intimidating technology/scale designed for children, (2) safety from tampering/vandalism, (3) erratic electricity supply, and (4) easy installation and serviceability.

SOLUTION

The design of H2.0 gives this intimidating technology a human face for use in schools. The design language of 'serious play' combines play with technology, tempering its authoritative power. The flat, rigid planes give a robust, powerful look. But its reassuring bulk is balanced with playful colours and graphics, making it comfortable to use for young users.

The knock-down and weld-free assembly, on the other hand, helps with easy installation. Locking mechanisms for critical components provide protection against vandalism, and gas spring hinges add to easy serviceability. The product runs on renewable/solar energy, circumventing power disruption and bringing reliability to the solution.

CLIENT SPEAK

Future Factory operates across the product development process, which helps build project success. They have a valuable blend of business, design and technology, which creates a useful perspective, and is unique in this space.

The reason we benefit from interaction with (the team) is that they bring in design talent, but with hard-core manufacturing expertise. So it's not just about a shape but also about its realization. We've had some experience with them and they have brought some very brilliant, economical and very beneficial ideas to our customers.

ABOUT THE DESIGN FIRM

Future Factory helps businesses succeed through innovation and design. Organized across 3 divisions, Strategy & Innovation, Design and Development, we engage with clients across the width of product development. Within these divisions, specialized capabilities reduce risk, pushing the boundaries of design. Working with health-care, consumer and industrial businesses, we are the partner you can expect more from.

SERVICES

- Research
- Strategy
- Innovation
- Industrial design
- Engineering
- Prototyping
- Vendor development
- Batch production

A55, Nandjyot Industrial Estate,
Safed Pool, Saki Naka,
Andheri (E), Mumbai 400 072

Geetika Kambli

+91 22 2859 6358 / +91 22 2859 4394

geetika@futurefactory.in

www.futurefactory.in

SMART CIRCUIT

PLC controlled circuit along with LCD display integrates the process parameters + makes self-diagnostics, predictive maintenance, data retrieval and review simpler.

DESIGN EXPERIENCE

The design language of "serious play", combines play with technology tempering it's authoritative power, and fostering a close relationship with the school community. It is also enhanced through careful detailing Here, customised push nozzles help build playful interaction.

EXQUISITE ENGINEERING

Knock down + Weld free assembly offering on-location assembly convenience. H2.0 is designed to run on renewable energy / solar, working independently with PLC controlled technology.

Design Firm:
Godrej & Boyce Mfg Co. Ltd — Appliance Division

Project:
Godrej Glitz Fully Automatic Washing Machine Range

Design Team:
Suhas Kulkarni, Mohan Kumar, Ashok H., Jayesh Sawant, and Futuring Design
Mentor: Mr B. J. Wadia

PROJECT TITLE

Development of a fully automatic washing machine of capacity upto 7 kg, offering better laundry wash and convenience in use.

BACKGROUND

Consumers from the age group of 25–45 years, from metro cities, aspiring to upgrade from a semi-auto washer to a feature-loaded automatic washer, expect good washing quality and user convenience. This needs a machine with effective cleaning and features offering more convenience.

CHALLENGE

Laundry users today have no special aid to remove tough stains on cuffs and collars. In India, interrupted water or power supply disrupt laundry washing. Offering a special cleaning method with user-friendly features at an affordable cost is challenging.

SOLUTION

Patented U-Sonic technology in the Glitz washing machine helps remove tough stains on cuffs and collars. The patented Dynamic Aqua Power Control completes the washing cycle even when water and power are available intermittently. The clothes-load indicator helps indicate the overloading of clothes, which deters washing quality. The powerful aqua-jet pulsator, gravity drum and the built-in water heater enable good and hygienic cleaning of laundry.

Among automatic washers, Glitz offers a better and more user-convenient laundry-washing experience, considering the prevalent water and power conditions in India. The availability of two capacities and a colour range makes it a worthy choice for meeting the demands of Indian consumers.

GOOD DESIGN

DESIGNED FOR THE INDIAN CONSUMER

Removes tough stains on cuffs and collars without use of harmfull chemicals : **U-Sonic**.

Relieves consumer of mental stress from worrying about electricity or water supply : **DAC**

CLIENT SPEAK

Key insights and relevant solutions evolved through consumer research are :
Ultrasonic aids effective cleaning for cuffs and collars, reducing user effort and fabric damage.
DAC offers complete laundry-washing cycle without user intervention, in spite of intermittent supply of water and power.
Improved viewing experience of effective washing is given to the user by curved glass and a tilted control panel.

ABOUT THE DESIGN TEAM

The Glitz range of washing machines is a result of deploying patented technologies that offer immense user convenience and product features that ensure good and hygienic washing quality. The in-house engineering expertise of technology, testing and manufacturing along with product styling by Futuring Design with the support of the in-house industrial design team, put together a technologically and aesthetically winning product.

Godrej & Boyce Mfg Co. Ltd
Pirojshanagar, Vikhroli,
Mumbai 400 079, Maharashtra

Mr Suhas Kulkarni

+91 22 6796 6361,
+91 22 6796 6364

rtone@godrej.com

www.godrejappliances.com

PIONEERING TECHNOLOGIES FOR USER CONVENIENCE

*ULTRA SONIC STAIN REMOVER

By forming waves of nano bubble, it improves washing, especially tough stains on cuffs and collars. Unmatched by any other competitor *(Patented*)*.

*DYNAMIC AQUA CONTROL (DAC) TECHNOLOGY

Allows the user to set the wash cycle even in absence of power/water supply - an unmatched patented technology feature.

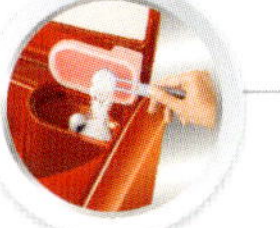

DETERGENT MIXER

Ensures uniform mixing of detergent with water, this avoids soap lumps which are otherwise seen on washed clothes.

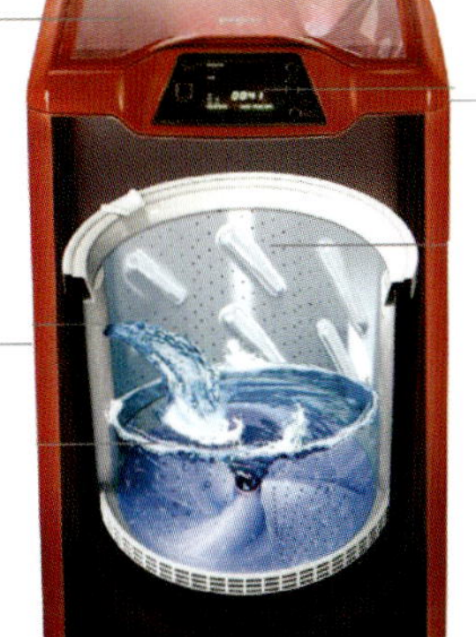

DIGITAL CONTROL PANEL

Design Firm:
Godrej & Boyce Mfg Co. Ltd — Appliance Division

Project:
Godrej Edge Digi Direct-Cool Refrigerator Range

Design Team:
Suhas Kulkarni, Bhasker Panyam, Vijay Mahajan, Yohan Engineer and Future Factory LLP
Mentor: Mr B.J. Wadia

PROJECT TITLE

Development of direct-cool refrigerators, providing user convenience alike; frost-free refrigerator with the best-in-class energy rating.

BACKGROUND

Today, the Indian consumer aspires for frost-free refrigerators. However, intermittent power cuts compel users to buy direct-cool refrigerators as they have higher cooling retention during power cuts. Hence, there evolved a need for a cost-effective direct-cool refrigerator with the convenience of a frost-free refrigerator.

CHALLENGE

Developing a cost-effective, digitally controlled appliance operating under harsh Indian conditions for a highly cost-sensitive direct-cool consumer segment was a challenge. This meant making the refrigerator the most energy-efficient one, while delivering the best cooling efficiency and automated defrost like a frost-free.

SOLUTION

Through digital monitoring, it senses ambient light, usage pattern and controls the compressor function accordingly, making it the only hybrid refrigerator in India. It also has unique features like the door-mounted vegetable tray and cooling retention with 'Stay Cool' technology. Unlike any other conventional outward convex-shaped doors, Edge Digi is stylized with concave surface modulation on the door design, bringing out the character of a technologically advanced product in its form and styling.

Based on direct-cooling technology, Edge Digi proves to be the best product in its category in the Indian market In terms of user convenience, energy efficiency (6-star equivalent) and its aesthetic appeal.

INDIA'S 1ST HYBRID REFRIGERATOR
WITH FROST-FREE MODE

ENVIRONMENT FRIENDLY

HIGH ENERGY EFFICIENCY
WITH 6 STAR PERFORMANCE

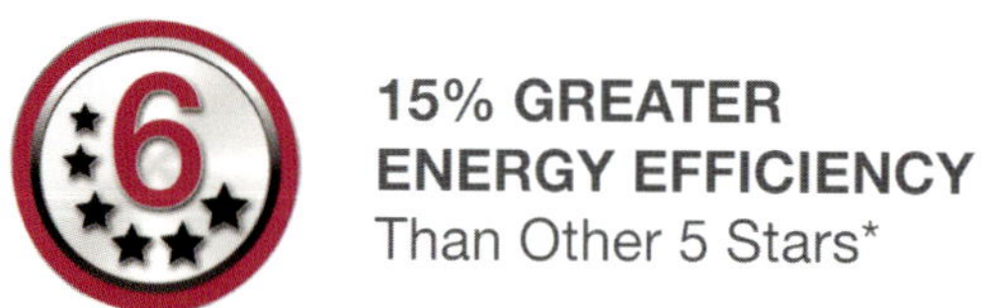

HIGHEST WARRANTY

CLIENT SPEAK

Insights and relevant innovations generated through consumer research are:

1: A digitally programmed auto-defrost to enable product usage considering the frequent power cuts in India.

2: Best-in-class energy efficiency aided through a digitally controlled compressor, satisfying the cost concerns of the user.

3: Provision of the largest vegetable tray in the direct-cool category, as it was observed to be the most utilized component.

ABOUT THE DESIGN TEAM

The Edge Digi refrigerator is a blend of innovative engineering and pleasing aesthetics. The in-house engineering expertise in cooling technology, testing and manufacturing and product styling by Future Factory LLP, along with the in-house industrial design team, resulted in a technologically evolved and aesthetically appealing product. Edge Digi has proved to be a success story for Godrej Appliances.

Godrej & Boyce Mfg Co. Ltd
Pirojshanagar, Vikhroli,
Mumbai 400 079, Maharashtra

Mr Suhas Kulkarni

+91 22 6796 6361,
+91 22 6796 6364

rtone@godrej.com

www.godrejappliances.com

Range Of Edge Digi Direct Cool Refrigerators

SKMD

Design Firm:
SKM Designs Private Limited

Project:
Solar Power Generator

Client:
IDT Consulting and Services, Inc., Dublin, California, USA

Design Team:
Industrial Designer: Sudhir Kumar
Mechanical Engineer: Anchit Saxena
Mechanical Engineer: Shashank Pandey
Prototype: Sanjay Sharma
Production: Jitendra Sharma

PROJECT TITLE

Design and prototype development of a solar power generator for any individual in urban or rural areas, at any location, for his basic electrical energy needs.

BACKGROUND

Solar power generators are being used widely on a larger scale and are very successful in power generation. They are gaining popularity, and every country has some good target to meet. When it comes to the use and acceptance of solar power generators for a single individual, the availability of the right product, purpose and affordability become an issue.

CHALLENGE

A major challenge was to zero down on the capacity, format and construction of the power generator. Power consumption varies for users in different locations and users belonging to different age groups.

SOLUTION

The solar power generator has been built around small and compact components like the high-efficient solar photovoltaic panel of 40W, a battery charge controller for charging lithium ion battery, a pure sine wave inverter of 300W and high power lithium ion battery of 11.1V Dc 30000mAH. All the components are compact and light in weight, especially the battery, which is 1/4th the size and 5 times lighter than a lead acid batter y for the storage rating.

An average 40W solar panel generates 40W of electrical energy at 12V DC which is sufficient to charge the lithium ion battery through charge controllers that are designed for the battery chemistry. A 300W pure sine wave inverter converts 12V DC to 220V/110V AC and can give 250W of electrical energy. This is sufficient enough to power several of the devices like an incandescent bulb, CFL, LED, tube lights, ceiling and pedestal fans, laptops, etc. Since the power output is 220/110V AC, any normal household device that consumes 50W or less can be run very efficiently.

WHAT ALL IT CAN RUN

any device that consumes 50W or lesser could be an ideal load. . .

and many more . . .

PLACE OF USE

and many more . . .

KEY FEATURES

SOLAR PHOTO VOLTAIC
40W SOLAR PANEL

INVERTER 300W
PURE SINE WAVE 110V/220V AC

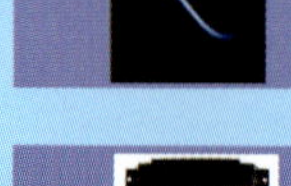

CHARGE CONTROLLER
FOR LITHIUM ION AND LEAD ACID

LITHIUM ION BATTERY
12V DC, 30000mAH

WEIGHT <10 KGs
LIGHT IN WEIGHT

COMPACT DESIGN
SMALLEST PRODUCT FOR POWER

MULTI-USE
USE BY ANYONE, ANYWHERE

PORTABLE
SINGLE PERSON PORTABILITY

UNIT COST
MODERATE

WARRANTY
STANDARD

INDIGENOUS
DESIGNED IN INDIA
MADE IN INDIA

CLIENT SPEAK

"The essence of the system is its compactness and ease of use. Affordable pricing with minimum preparation prior to its use add to its acceptance by any user, anywhere on this globe. This brings in smartness and makes the user feel pride in using free, abundant solar energy.

SERVICES

SKM Designs Pvt. Ltd is a hard-core industrial design consultancy firm located in Faridabad that has been creating innovative yet realistic design solutions for a diverse range of sectors, ranging from renewable energy, R & D, technology, appliances, and medical to consumer products, machines and environments. We have deep concern for the limited resources our planet has, and their depletion. We identify the problem, innovate to get an appropriate design solution and convert that into usable products. Our success has been founded on three key principles: originality, reliability and talent.

18A/2, DLF Industrial Estate, Phase-1
Faridabad 121003, Haryana

Sudhir Kumar, Director & Industrial Designer
Anand Vijay, Director-Global Management and Strategic Development

+91 129 4061280,
+91 93122 65178, +91 98102 73269

sudhir@skm-designs.com

www.skm-designs.com

SOLAR POWER GENERATOR

Design Firm:
Tanishq Design Studio

Project:
Inara

Client:
Titan Company Ltd, Jewellery Division

Design Team:
Tanishq Design Studio

CII DESIGN EXCELLENCE AWARDS 2014

PROJECT TITLE

Inara — Inspired from the underwater world

BACKGROUND

Inspired from coral, shells, sea creatures, fins, scales and skin patterns, this collection is high on design. The collection is judiciously designed to give a large spread at a relatively low price, using innovative illusion settings.

CHALLENGE

The biggest challenge was to give a large spread at a relatively lower diamond caratage and price, to offer the customer a true value-for-money product. New modular techniques envisaged for the collection were difficult to establish.

SOLUTION

It appeared impossible to give a large spread and yet bring down the diamond caratage. A lot of R&D was done to establish the illusion techniques required to give this effect. CNC cut, mirror-finished metal plates were identified to be best mimicking the diamond facets, which when set with a smaller diamond in the centre, creates an illusion of a much bigger diamond, hence giving a high perceived value. Another design marvel is the prudent usage of these illusion techniques in a way that it retains the preciousness of diamond jewellery, which otherwise may have looked gimmicky and cheap.

In Inara, various illusion techniques were mixed together along with regular diamond settings in a way that both complement the other. Illusion plates have been judiciously used along with prong and pave elements in a way that the look is not compromised. Inspired by an ostentatious theme like the underwater world, this collection is high on design.

DESIGNOMICS AWARDS 2013

STARS OF THE INDUSTRY AWARDS

CLIENT SPEAK

Inara explores modularity in a way that has never been tried in the category, offering necklaces that can be worn in 2–3 different looks as per the occasion, or as part of a necklace that can become a day-wear pendant or a cocktail pendant. Inara has reinforced the design leadership of Tanishq in the industry.

ABOUT THE DESIGN FIRM

Titan Company, established in 1984 as a joint venture between Tata and TNIDC, diversified in 1995 into jewellery to capitalize on a fragmented market under the brand name of Tanishq. Since then, Tanishq has emerged as the most desirable jewellery brand for the design-seeking, progressive Indian woman.

SERVICES

Jewellery Retail

No. 132/133, Divyasree Technopolis,
Off HAL Airport Road, Yamlur Post,
Yamlur, Bengaluru 560 037, Karnataka

Chandrakala

+91 80 6660 9537

kala@titan.co.in

www.titan.co.in

Features

Contemporary styling balancing negative and positive areas

Innovative Illusion setting techniques

Dancing diamond

Faceted plates

Modularity

Design Firm:
Global Consumer Design,
Whirlpool of India Ltd

Project:
Whirlpool's Protton World Series Refrigerators

Design Team:
Suresh Sethi, Sumit Singh, Ashish Gupta, Varun Suri, Prashant Sharma, Tanya Dhanny, Eshaa Venkatesh, Anannya Patra

PROJECT TITLE

Whirlpool introduces Protton World Series Refrigerators. Because urban lifestyles are changing.

BACKGROUND

Protton World Series is a smart, new entrant in the world of refrigerators. The latest from Whirlpool, Protton is a three-door, top-mount and frost-free refrigerator. Its unique design makes for elegant looks and highly differentiated door aesthetics.

CHALLENGE

Modern, convenience-led lifestyles have led to new consumption patterns. Vegetables are bought for the week. Thus, storage, long-lasting freshness, preventing cooling loss due to door opening and odour mixing are the key consumer needs. Protton World Series has been designed keeping such considerations in mind.

SOLUTION

The Protton World Series redefines freshness standards with its 6th-Sense Active Fresh Technology. It also introduces a unique combination of format — a dedicated separate drawer for vegetables, with the largest crisper (35.5L) in its range. The exclusive vegetable drawer works beautifully to prevent odour mixing and reduces cooling loss due to frequent door-opening.

The Protton World Series boasts of international design inputs, inspired by the 'Island approach', Whirlpool's Global Visual Brand Language. This gives the Protton World Series an integrated handle and user interface for a streamlined and flush appearance. As a result, all interaction areas of the product get grouped into one clear point of focus.

DESIGNOMICS AWARDS 2014

GOOD DESIGN

CLIENT SPEAK

'If something fulfills function, it has inherent beauty'—Socrates

The Protton World Series' flush-door aesthetics is a clear illustration of the above statement. Its attractive looks are perfectly complemented by amazing functionality. Designed for compact, modern kitchens, it takes less space while door opening. This product has been awarded the Good Design Award, the India Design Mark 2014, and the Gold Award at Designomics 2014.

ABOUT THE DESIGN FIRM

Global Consumer Design (GCD) is Whirlpool's in-house design function and innovation driver. The team comprises experts from diverse backgrounds like industrial, graphics, usability, colour material finish (CFM) and interaction design. GCD's design vision reflects a 'global but local' approach. Innovative yet balanced by an understanding of consumers, seeking 'real-life' insights are the raison d'être of Whirlpool's design.

KEY PROJECT FEATURES

- Progressive and flushed-door aesthetics
- Largest vegetable drawer (35.5L) in its range
- Air-booster system
- High moisture retention technology (HMRT)
- 'Freshkeeper' in vegetable compartment absorbs harmful gases
- Anti-bacterial additive, 'Microblock'
- Consumes energy less than a CFL bulb

Global Consumer Design
Whirlpool House, Plot No. 40,
Sector 44, Gurgaon 122 002, Haryana

Mr Suresh Sethi

+91 124 4591300
+91 124 4591301

suresh_sethi@whirlpool.com

www.whirlpoolindia.com

Design Firm:
Global Consumer Design,
Whirlpool of India Ltd

Project:
Whirlpool's Superb Atom Washing Machine

Design Team:
Suresh Sethi, Anand Asinkar, Rohtash Kumar, Varun Suri, Prashant Sharma, Tanya Dhanny, Eshaa Venkatesh, Anannya Patra

PROJECT TITLE

Whirlpool's Superb Atom Washing Machine. A triumph of design.

BACKGROUND

Superb Atom is the latest innovation in semi-automatic washing machines from Whirlpool. With its ease of use, aesthetics and convenience, it has the makings of a real winner. With Superb Atom, Whirlpool has once again proven that its innovative products are game changers in all segments.

CHALLENGE

Superb Atom addresses two main challenges. Firstly, shrinking home sizes needed compactness, and secondly, the entry segment needed washing of cuffs and collars by hand.

SOLUTION

Design Convenience: Washing clothes is a demanding, physical chore. Superb Atom makes it easier. Top scrub surface with dots means no bending while scrubbing. Form: Shaped like a bathtub with soft curves, it merges with other bathroom installations. Size perception: The lids extend across the entire footprint, directing the eye to the top of the machine. Organization of elements: Unlike conventional designs, the control panel for the first time ever, has been shifted to the left (wash side), and at the same time is also flush with the top. This adds to the international look. Manufacturing: The D-shape and subtle curves on the body make this machine the most economical to manufacture.

CLIENT SPEAK

'Recognizing the need is the primary condition for design'—Charles Eames

Superb Atom reflects a holistic approach to design. It integrates consumer benefits with craftsmanship, usability with best manufacturability, optimum size with foremost good aesthetics. For Whirlpool, the role of design has probably been the most influential in Superb Atom. It has proved that design as a function can work to integrate all processes to create a winning product.

ABOUT THE DESIGN FIRM

Global Consumer Design (GCD) is Whirlpool's in-house design function and innovation driver. The team comprises experts from diverse backgrounds like industrial, graphics, usability, colour material finish (CFM) and interaction design. GCD's design vision reflects a 'global but local' approach. Innovative yet balanced by an understanding of consumers, seeking 'real-life' insights are the raison d'être of Whirlpool's design.

KEY PROJECT FEATURES

- 'D-Shape' seen for the first time ever in washing machines
- Scrub surface on top with water-draining design
- First-time-ever non-projecting control panel
- Waterproof control panel with knob inset design
- Multi-utility tray with the wash lid
- Largest spin & wash lids in the segment
- Least cost of manufacturing due to shape
- Auto-restart for wash cycle (in case of electricity loss)

Global Consumer Design
Whirlpool House, Plot No. 40,
Sector 44, Gurgaon 122 002, Haryana

Mr Suresh Sethi

+91 124 4591300
+91 124 4591301

suresh_sethi@whirlpool.com

www.whirlpoolindia.com

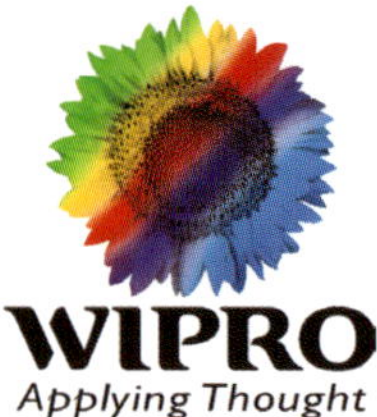

Design Firm:
Wipro Furniture Business

Project:
OnAir

Design Team:
I + D Studio

PROJECT TITLE

OnAir

BACKGROUND

OnAir is a simple, stylish and sophisticated task chair which combines excellent comfort, support, aesthetics, functionality and intuitive adjustability.

CHALLENGE

OnAir is a task chair that is designed to create an emotional connect and ownership among the users towards the chair in an otherwise impersonal environment. Chairs are mostly designed like machines. OnAir breaks this mould through the innovative design that combines engineered functionality with emotional connectivity.

SOLUTION

OnAir encompasses all that a task chair should represent. It redefines the visual language of a task chair through amalgamation of all functions into an integrated form leading to its iconic character. The distinctive plastic-shell back is seamlessly integrated with versatile armrests and adjustable lumber support. OnAir is generously proportioned to improve the comfort of seating for all percentiles. With a very contemporary and sharp shape, OnAir is a contemporary expression of the contemporary task chair. The auto-adjusting mechanism adjusts the back tension according to the user's weight, making the experience more comfortable without any manual intervention.

CLIENT SPEAK

Most task chairs have a machine-like appearance with complicated controls. Users are unaware of functions and their controls, and end up using them with the wrong settings, leading to health issues. We decided to design a chair that is simple, sleek, stylish and intuitive in its use, and which self-adjusts to the user's weight and is affordable for cost-conscious Indian buyers.

ABOUT THE DESIGN FIRM

The WIPRO Furniture team has always been driven by their innate passion to innovate and their absolute dedication to achieving excellence in design. I+D Studio, which stands for 'Innovation + Design Studio', is the culmination of this thought process. Innovative thinking, thoughtful design, a user-centric approach and critical execution are the factors behind the success of our products.

#134 Doddakannelli, Sarjapur Road,
Next to Wipro Corporate Office,
Bangalore 560 035, Karnataka

Mr Vipul Kumar, Mr Nataraju Shiva

+91 80 9991 8190

vipul.kumar1@wipro.com
nataraju.shiva@wipro.com

www.wiprofurniturebusiness.com

Design Firm:
Wipro Furniture Business

Project:
EMBASSY

Design Team:
I + D Studio

PROJECT TITLE

PRESIDENCY: Executive office suites

BACKGROUND

PRESIDENCY is an executive furniture range with contemporary design. The dual finish of the main table creates an interesting contrast. The fusion of the contemporary look and feel with its voluminous sturdy design makes it an appropriate choice for any office.

CHALLENGE

PRESIDENCY is designed keeping in mind the entrepreneurs and business owners who have been using carpentered furniture which relies on the skills and materials used. PRESIDENCY is made to overcome these challenges and improve the image of mass-produced furniture.

SOLUTION

PRESIDENCY is very sturdy and stable. It has a thick tabletop and a gable end that is made of superior material. The form of the product is asymmetric and contemporary, which sets it apart in terms of visual appeal. The main table has dual finishes, creating an interesting contrast. The full-height modesty is keeping in mind the sensitivity these users have towards privacy. The inbuilt flip-top box, DUO, enables the user to access power and data easily. The various offerings, viz. the main table, return table extension table, are available in multiple sizes, which allows them to be used in any layout.

CLIENT SPEAK

PRESIDENCY is designed for a segment which still supports a certain hierarchy. Mostly, it will be used in the manager's cabin or in the proprietor's office, and the voluminous yet contemporary look of PRESIDENCY will help users to maintain their hierarchy. The various offerings also allow users to set multiple variants of layouts.

ABOUT THE DESIGN FIRM

The WIPRO Furniture team has always been driven by their innate passion to innovate and their absolute dedication to achieving excellence in design. I+D Studio, which stands for 'Innovation + Design Studio', is the culmination of this thought process. Innovative thinking, thoughtful design, a user-centric approach and critical execution are the factors behind the success of our products.

#134 Doddakannelli, Sarjapur Road,
Next to Wipro Corporate Office,
Bangalore 560 035, Karnataka

Mr Vipul Kumar, Mr Nataraju Shiva

+91 80 9991 8190

vipul.kumar1@wipro.com
nataraju.shiva@wipro.com

www.wiprofurniturebusiness.com

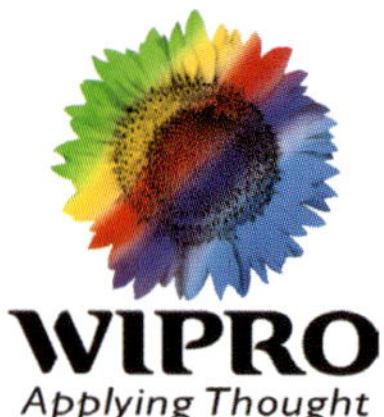

Design Firm:
Wipro Furniture Business

Project:
XCEED

Design Team:
I + D Studio

PROJECT TITLE

XCEED

BACKGROUND

Xceed is a modular solution for small enterprises, start-ups and branch offices. Inspired by the Indian work culture of 'achieving more with less', it is flexible enough to fit into any layout. It enables interior designers to upgrade to a knock-down installation-friendly system.

CHALLENGE

Small enterprises, start-up companies and small branch-offices rely mostly on carpenters for a customized solution, which is dependent on the skill set of the carpenter, and is prone to an inconsistent finish, limited material variety and budget escalations.

SOLUTION

Xceed bridges the gap between customized interior and modular offices. It enables carpenters to upgrade to a modular-furniture concept using Xceed, which is completely knock-down, modular, can be easily assembled on-site and can complement any office interior. The major advantages of Xceed are its flexibility to fit into different spaces, adaptability to suit different work patterns, ease of execution, easy and convenient maintenance and, above all, the trust and assurance of quality. All these advantages make Xceed the perfect choice for small offices which aspire to own a modular office.

CLIENT SPEAK

The most important characteristic of Xceed is its adaptability. Most modular furniture systems are not adaptable and cannot be altered to suit specific needs. Xceed achieves this with simple yet innovative detailing. The sliding bracket that connects the tabletop to the pedestal makes it possible to expand the benching arrangement to fit the space without adding any components.

ABOUT THE DESIGN FIRM

The WIPRO Furniture team has always been driven by their innate passion to innovate and their absolute dedication to achieving excellence in design. I+D Studio, which stands for 'Innovation + Design Studio', is the culmination of this thought process. Innovative thinking, thoughtful design, a user-centric approach and critical execution are the factors behind the success of our products.

#134 Doddakannelli, Sarjapur Road,
Next to Wipro Corporate Office,
Bangalore 560 035, Karnataka

Mr Vipul Kumar, Mr Nataraju Shiva

+91 80 9991 8190

vipul.kumar1@wipro.com
nataraju.shiva@wipro.com

www.wiprofurniturebusiness.com

Design Firm:
Advandes Design Engineering Services LLP

Project:
Water -Tank Design

Client:
M/s Shree Hardeo Industries

Design Team:
Mr Sanket Kothekar, Mr Akash Mitra,
Mr Bhupinder Pal Singh

ABOUT THE PROJECT

Water tanks are commonly noticed on the rooftops of independent houses and industrial areas. They are continuously exposed to harsh weather and heat. The design requirement is to have a desirable yet sturdy water-tank in the market to compete with the best of industry. The project outcome is that there is now a range of water tanks with capacity from 500L to 2000L.

KEY FEATURES

- The design is inspired from the waves in water
- The design language is adapted on the cap. The feature helps the user to have a firm grip to open the cap
- The new design with wave-shaped structural ribs has helped save material without compromising on strength
- Four-ply blow moulding enables the rigidity for bearing higher volumes of water
- Product branding was made prominent by distinct colour and embossed letters

F-3, 1103 / 1-15, Ulhas Govind Apartments
Model Colony, Pune 411 016, Maharashtra

Mr Satish Komaragiri

+91 99605 03550

satish@advandes.com

www.advandes.com

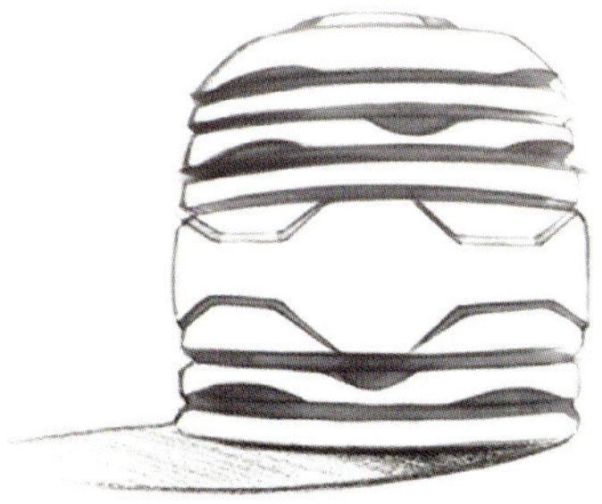

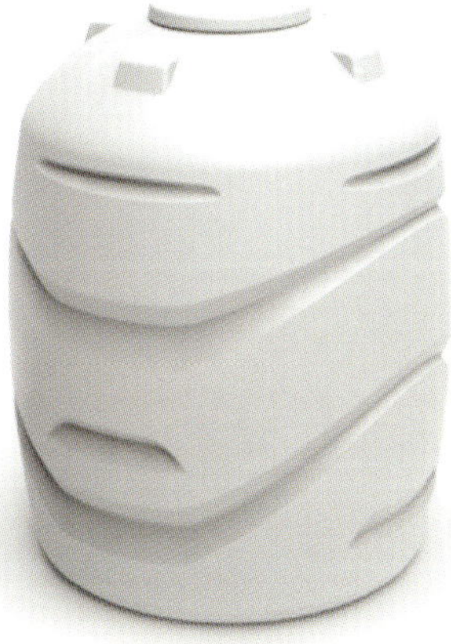

500L

750L

1000L

1500L

2000L

Design Firm:
Advandes Design Engineering Services LLP

Project:
Bottle-Top Dispenser

Client:
Microlit

Design Team:
Mr Atul Jain (Microlit)
Mr Sreejith Kumar P. S. (Advandes)
Mr Satish Mudhalkar (Advandes)

ABOUT THE PROJECT

Microlit approached Advandes to design their new bottle-top dispenser for liquid dispensing in scientific laboratories. The challenge was to engineer intricate assembly while maintaining the accuracy for fluid dispensing and usability requirements in a lab environment. This equipment has good export potential due to the quality and economy that India offers to the world. This product was successfully launched at MEDICA 2014, Dusseldorf, in Germany, and has won much appreciation.

KEY FEATURES

- Sharp features to depict accuracy that the instrument provides
- Ergonomically designed knobs and body
- Quick-release slider mechanism for volume setting
- Aesthetics drawn from the function aspects of the product
- Flexible outlet designed for product packaging and assembly
- Scratch-proof printing for durability of calibration

F-3, 1103 / 1-15, Ulhas Govind Apartments, Model Colony, Pune 411 016, Maharashtra

Sreejith Kumar P.S. (Advandes)

+91 90999 09250

sreejith@advandes.com

www.advandes.com

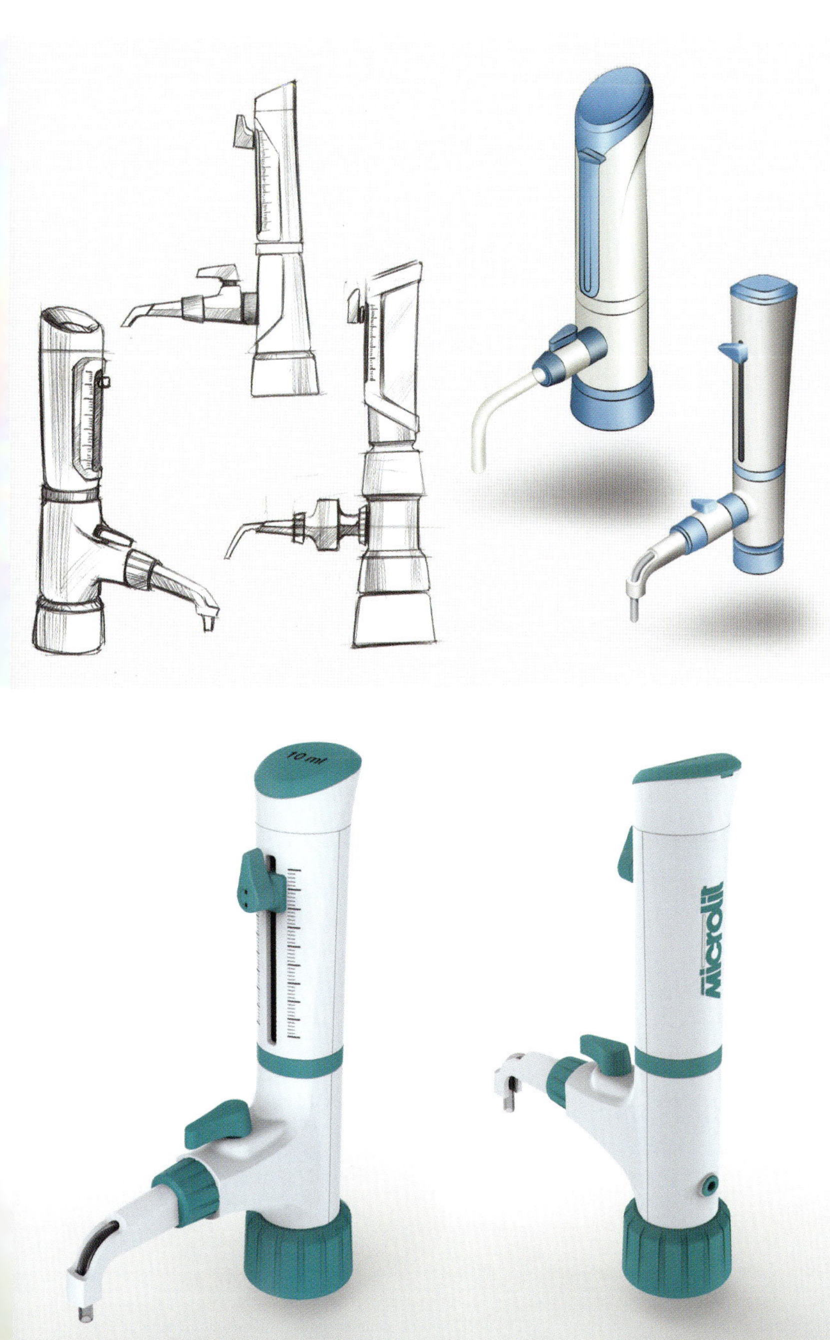

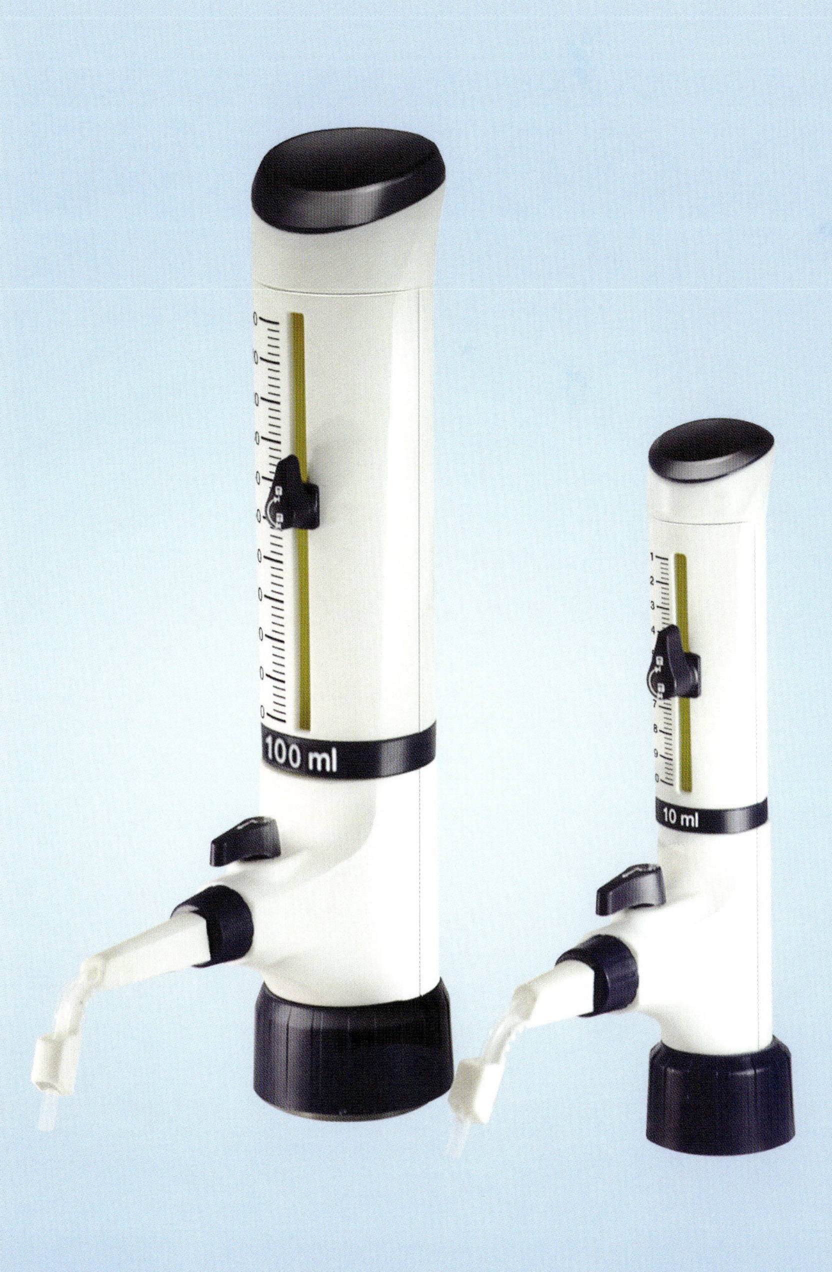

Company Name:
Carborundum Universal Limited (designed and crafted by 'The Ceramic Arts (TCA)', the in-house unit of CUMI, Murugappa Group that explores the aesthetic dimension of inventive materials like zirconia, alumina ceramics, etc.)

Project:
Murugappa Star Performer Award (MSPA) design

Design Team:
Ms Bhavya Kamalia

ABOUT THE PROJECT

The Murugappa Star Performer Award is presented to the best-performing companies within the Murugappa Group every year. The design brief brought the challenge to craft a unique, iconic and substantive award that is readily identifiable with the Group. Taking its inspiration from the Murugappa Logo, the overall form, artwork and choice of material personify the spirit of the award.

KEY FEATURES

- Overall form is crafted in high alumina ceramics
- The ceramic is metallized to create the artwork and then plated in 24k gold
- The eye is a red Swarovski crystal

Industrial Ceramics Division, 47 & 48 (Part), Sipcot Industrial Complex, Hosur 635 126, Tamil Nadu

Ms Bhavya Kamalia

+91 76764 44799, 04344 304700

theceramicarts@gmail.com

www.facebook.com/TheCeramicArts

Design Firm:
Cluster One Creative Solutions Pvt. Ltd

Project:
Design of Snack-Bottle-Vending Machine

Client:
Chevend Technologies, Mumbai

Design Team:
Parag Sen & Parag Ainchwar

ABOUT THE PROJECT

The project was to design a snack–bottle vending machine as an alternative to imported machines. Enhanced product display and visibility, effective illumination and the retrieval bin with dispensed product visibility were important aspects of the brief. Noise reduction was part of the technology upgradation. The image below shows the first prototype installed for field trials.

KEY FEATURES

- Export market/import substitution
- Usability-led design
- New product retrieval system
- Partial refrigeration
- Styling
- Enhanced product display and illumination
- Note acceptor and coin changer
- Display screen for content dissemination

G-17, Gera Plaza, Boat Club Road,
Pune 411 001, Maharashtra

Mr Parag Sen

+91 98224 08714, +91 94220 13178

thecluster@cluster-one.net

www.cluster-one.net

DESIGNDIRECTIONS®

Design Company:
Design Directions Pvt. Ltd

Project:
MiraCradle™ — Neonate Cooler

Client:
Pluss Polymers Pvt. Ltd, Gurgaon

Design Team:
Satish Gokhale, Amol Patil

ABOUT THE PROJECT

The MiraCradle™ — Neonate Cooler is an affordable passive cooling device to induce therapeutic hypothermia among newborns suffering from birth asphyxia. It uses the advanced savE® Phase-Change Materials (PCMs), which are special thermal-energy storage materials that store and release heat at a particular temperature. It was launched in the market in August 2014.

KEY FEATURES

- Affordable solution to treat birth asphyxia
- Easy to use, safe, lightweight and portable
- Precise temperature control of 33–34°C upto 72 hours
- Costs just 1/10th of the present electronic devices
- Does not require a constant supply of electricity

828, Shivajinagar, 'Rajeev',
Bhandarkar Road, Lane #13,
Pune 411 004, Maharashtra

Mr Satish Gokhale

+91 20 2567 1941, +91 20 2565 3902

info@designdirections.net

www.designdirections.net

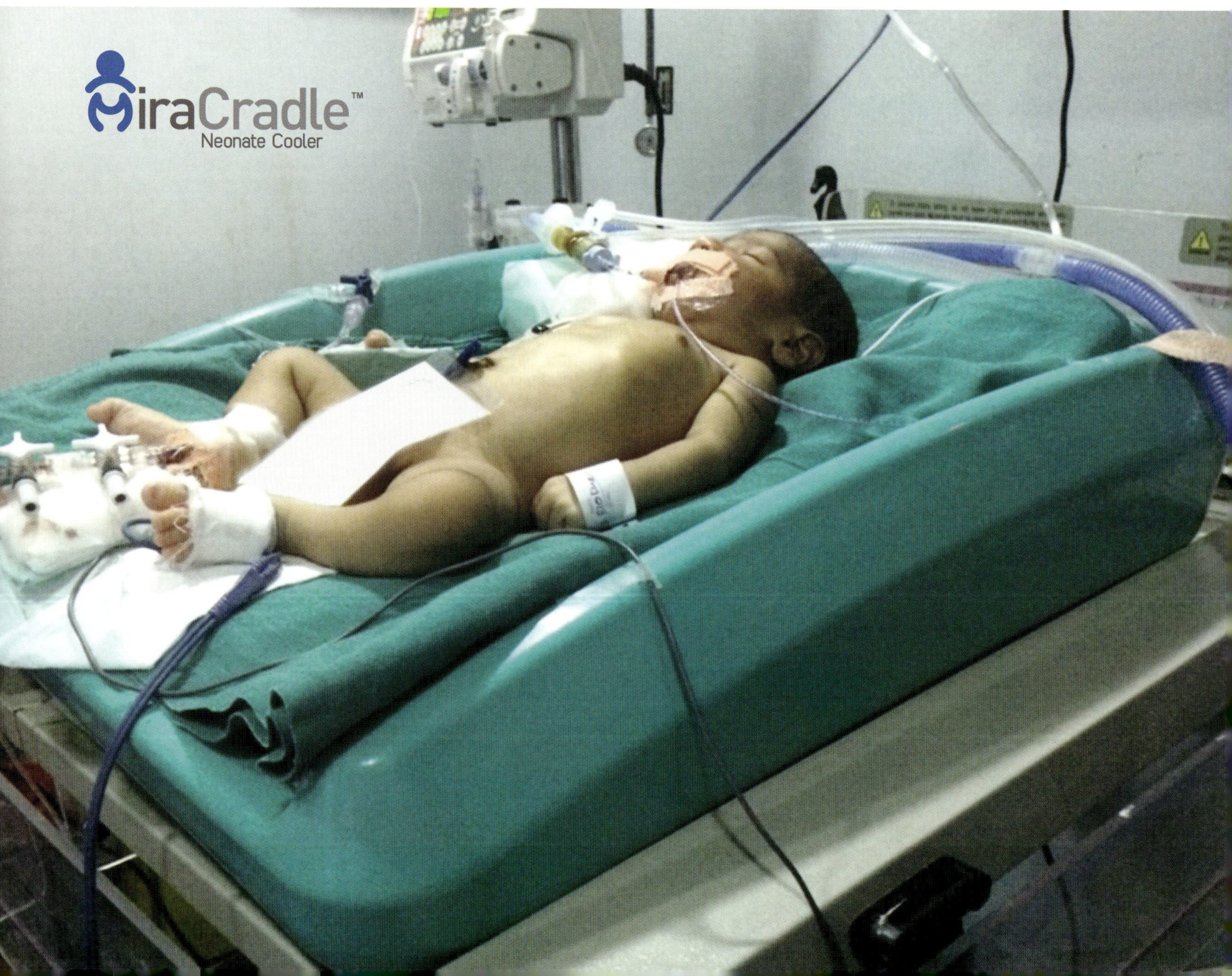

DESIGNDIRECTIONS®

ABOUT THE PROJECT

GroEzee is a kitchen vegetable-garden system for urban homes. It can be easily fitted in a balcony, terrace or a broad windowsill. GroEzee has an interconnected system to minimize the effort of watering every planter. GroEzee is designed such that the plants do not need watering for 5–6 days.

Design Firm:
Design Directions Pvt. Ltd

Project:
GroEzee Mobile Kitchen Garden Unit

Client:
Design Directions Pvt. Ltd

Design Team:
Satish Gokhale, Nachiket Gole, Sridhar Jaganathan

KEY FEATURES

- Continuous water supply to plants keeps them moist always
- Easy to maintain, water and move around
- 'Time-to-water-your plants' indicator
- Can grow a large variety of vegetable plants and microgreens
- Visually attractive

828, Shivajinagar, 'Rajeev',
Bhandarkar Road, Lane #13,
Pune 411 004, Maharashtra

Mr Satish Gokhale

+91 20 2565 3902 / +91 98220 40752

satish@designdirections.net

www.designdirections.net
www.groezee.com

Design Firm:
Designlipi Projects Pvt. Ltd

Project:
Eveready Ultra LED Lantern & Torchlight

Client:
Eveready Industries India Limited

Design Team:
Sanbid Golui & Team

CII DESIGN EXCELLENCE AWARDS 2014

ABOUT THE PROJECT

Eveready is a popular brand in rural and semi-urban India for torchlights and batteries. This project was a challenge to break the monotony of conventional product ranges with new features to increase the usage of the product with a larger functional benefit for the user, and to establish 'innovation' as a key brand lever for the brand Eveready.

KEY FEATURES

- This handy product is a self-standing lantern along with a torchlight with the same source of power
- This product has now became an essential & daily-use emergency light source from a limited-usage product like a torch
- Good product for fieldworkers, maintenance engineers, electricians, etc.
- Essential product for long-distance travel by road / car for emergency use
- Good utility product for rural / common toilet

Pencil Bhavan, Uttar Maju,
Maju Jagatballavpur, Howrah,
West Bengal 711 414

Mr Sanbid Golui

+91 98305 99955

sanbid@gmail.com

www.designlipi.com

DESMANIA

Design Firm:
Desmania

Project:
All-weather Smart AC

Client:
Voltas

Design Team:
Desmania Delhi

ABOUT THE PROJECT

Desmania partnered with Voltas to create the industry's leading smart split ACs on an all-weather platform. The endeavour was to create a unique brand language for Voltas, which carried over their legacy of trust, fused with the vibrancy of youth. The design thought-process was to achieve maximum return on the investment through an intelligent modular construction. The product caters to a large, pluralistic section of the market.

KEY FEATURES

- Three distinct-looking units at the cost of one
- Suction area on three sides of the front panel through design
- Smart sense: Adjusts according to the temperature outside
- Smart remote: Your phone is the remote

No. 4, Third Floor, Community Centre,
PVR Complex, Saket,
New Delhi 110 017, Delhi

Mr Anuj Prasad

+91 11 4176 5327,
+91 11 4100 9587

marketing@desmania.com

www.desmania.com

Three distinguished products can be derived out of changing just one component which contributes to 90% of product aesthetics ! In India where design preferences changes from place to place, culture to culture this design provides huge possibility for serving to niche markets with minimum investment

DESMANIA

Design Firm:
Desmania

Project:
Nescafé Solution

Client:
Nestlé Professional

Design Team:
Desmania Delhi

ABOUT THE PROJECT

Nescafé Solution was designed to bring a sense of sophistication to the dispensing machine and provide a rich experience to users consistent with the Nestlé brand. The design brief entailed a machine that would set the benchmark for beverage dispensers and would look relevant and contemporary even five years hence. After extensive research, various usage issues were highlighted, which were then analysed and interpreted through design by providing various new features.

KEY FEATURES

- Highly involving user experience
- Hygienic, illuminated dispensing area
- Easily wipeable flat, stainless-steel dispensing area
- Backlit LED logo
- Large, inviting interface
- Easily replaceable product list

No. 4, Third Floor, Community Centre,
PVR Complex, Saket,
New Delhi 110017, Delhi

Mr Anuj Prasad

+ 91 11 4176 5327,
+91 11 4100 9587

marketing@desmania.com

www.desmania.com

Nestlé PROFESSIONAL

Nescafé Solution

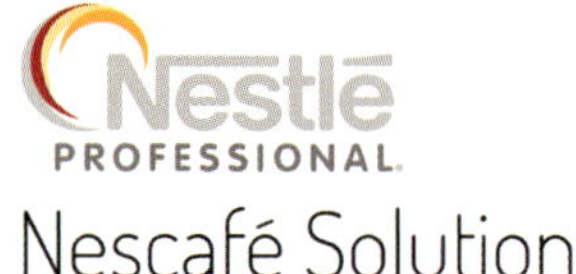

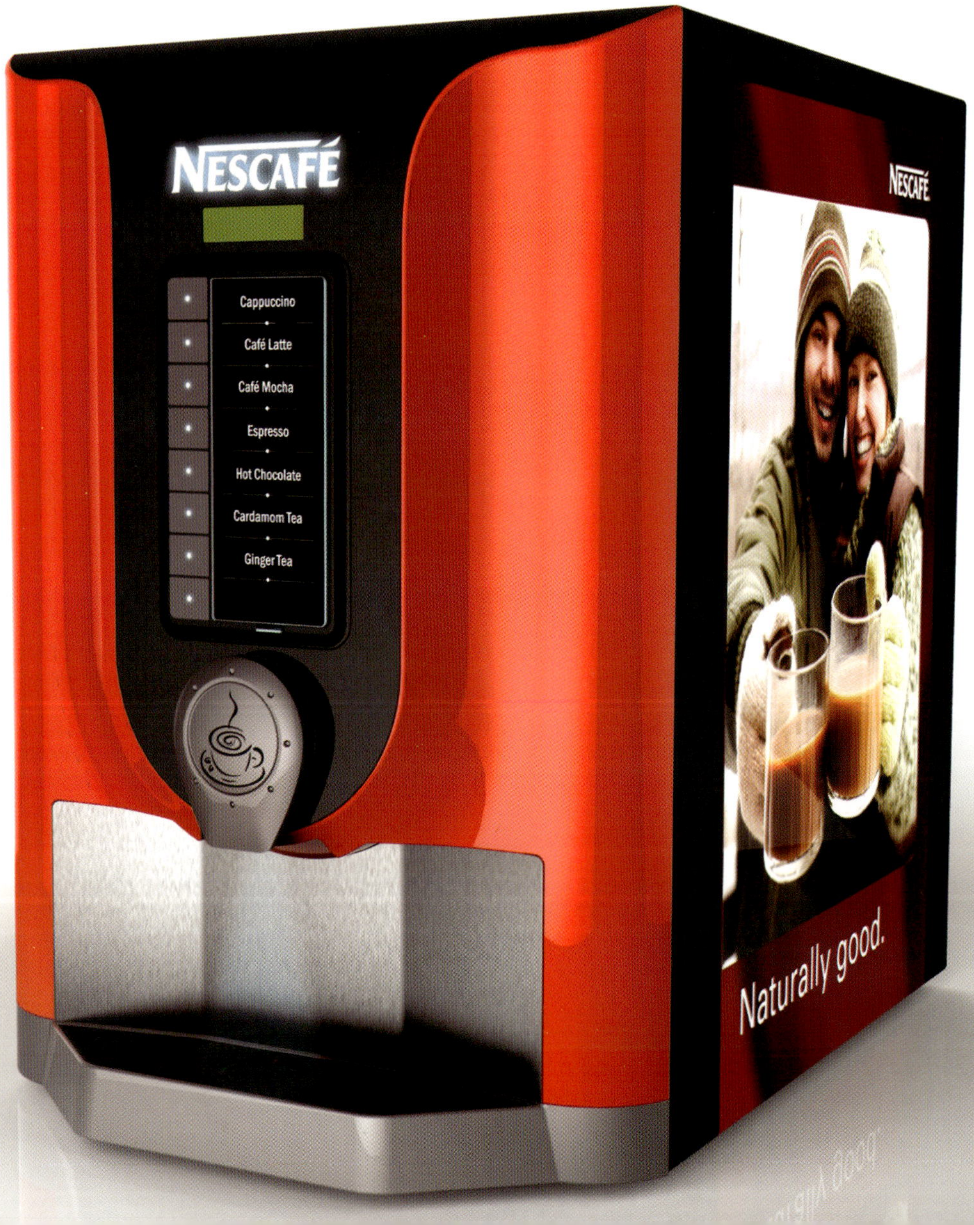

empoise

Design Firm:
Empoise Design Studios

Project:
Solar Home Light — SHL20

Client:
Luminous Power Technologies Pvt. Ltd

Design Team:
Saikat Biswas, Puttaraj Belaldavar

ABOUT THE PROJECT

Luminous SHL20 is a portable integrated solar-powered lighting system and DC power-pack, useful for semi-urban, rural and off-grid homes. This compact device can support two LED lights, a DC fan and has a built-in energy-efficient LED lamp. It can also charge mobile phones when there is no electricity available.

KEY FEATURES

- Compact and self-sufficient
- Portable power source
- Can be charged with solar panels or the AC
- Multiple DC outputs for LED lamps and DC Fan
- Built-in LED lamp with brightness control
- Can charge a phone without electricity line
- Robust and ergonomic design

#2, Chick Bazaar Road Cross,
Off Queens' Road,
Bangalore 560 051, Karnataka

Mr Saikat Biswas

+91 80 42198138

contact@empoise.com

www.empoise.com

foleydesigns

ABOUT THE PROJECT

Like ripples on the water surface, the Tiara is composed of several concentric circles that radiate outwards. The rings themselves provide grace and functionality while remaining a seamless, organic form. Designed to reflect dynamism, it creates an impression of a free-flow fluid. The faucet marries technological complexity with sculptural purity.

KEY FEATURES

- Play of ripples
- Seamless
- Crafted like jewellery
- Create a sense of dynamism
- Sense of mystique

Yolee — No. 14, 202, Second Floor,
Pottery Road, Richards Town,
Bangalore 560 005, Karnataka

Mr Nigel Foley

+91 97409 55774, +91 80 41540181 / 82

info@foleydesigns.com

www.foleydesigns.com

Design Firm:
Foley Designs Pvt. Ltd

Project:
Jaquar Faucet

Client:
JAQUAR

Design Team:
In-house Industrial Design Team

foleydesigns

ABOUT THE PROJECT

The HUL Pureit Marvella UV+Cold derives inspiration from minimalistic design language, enhancing the functionality of dispensing cold, pure water. The asymmetric treatment with elegant contours reinforces the dual nature of the device making it unique in its category. The compact, sleek design allows it to blend into modern kitchen spaces. The feather-touch buttons provide a rich user experience and interaction with the device.

KEY FEATURES

- Minimalistic design
- Elegant contours
- Unique in category
- Compact and sleek
- Feather-touch buttons

Yolee — No. 14, 202, Second Floor, Pottery Road, Richards Town, Bangalore 560 005, Karnataka

Mr Nigel Foley

+91 97409 55774, +91 80415 40181 / 82

info@foleydesigns.com

www.foleydesigns.com

Design Firm:
Foley Designs Pvt. Ltd

Project:
Pureit — Marvella UV + COLD

Client:
Hindustan Unilever

Design Team:
In-house Product Design Team

ABOUT THE PROJECT

Forbes Marshall Marshall B Packaged steam boiler is a three-pass wet-back automatic boiler system which can be found at the heart of any process industry. These boilers are 24x7 machines which provide a continuous supply of the driest steam steam, using the least amount of fuel and floor space.

KEY FEATURES

- Packaged boiler house system; plug and play system
- Compact design
- Modular design can be scaled
- Ergonomic, user-friendly design
- Strong visual aesthetics, brand

A-31, MIDC Estate, H Block, Pimpri,
Pune 411 018, Maharashtra

Mr Kunal Ghate

+91 93218 64814, +91 20 3985 1257

kghate@forbesmarshall.com

www.forbesmarshall.com

Design Firm:
Forbes Marshall Pvt. Ltd

Project:
Marshall B Boiler

Design Team:
Amod Gijare, Kunal Ghate, Kuldeep Yadav, Vijay Gorane

Bend Sheet

Intuitive control Panel

Pre-Wired

Pre-Insulated

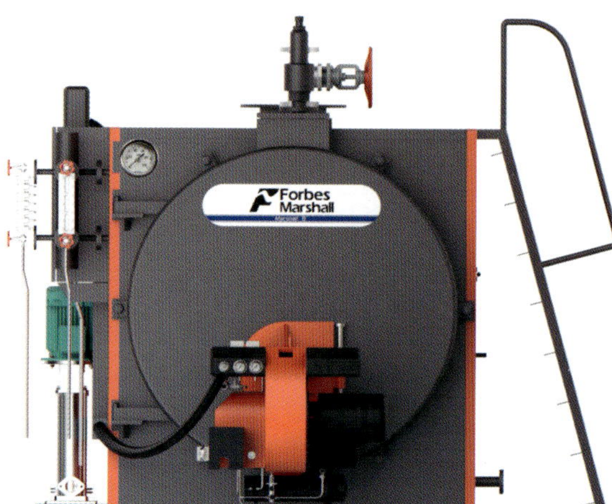

Design Company:
Future Factory

Project:
Magna — A smart water purifier

Client:
Eureka Forbes Limited

Design Team:
Jashish Kambli, Kunal Borkar

ABOUT THE PROJECT

Across the world, water has many sources and different impurities, but no single purifier addresses this disparity effectively. Magna is an innovation that uses a smart circuit to sense input water and apply different technologies in real-time, addressing impurities in changing input water — a first in this category.

KEY FEATURES

- Smart circuit: Intelligent application of technology to input water
- Formal quality: Flowing sensual surfaces; reassuring yet attractive
- Ergonomics: Compact design for tabletop and wall-mount options
- Serviceability: Screw-less design, easily removable panels
- Plug and play: Quick-fix connecters for easy installation
- Sustainability: 10 per cent water saving; 15 per cent less material used; biodegradable packaging

A55, Nandjyot Industrial Estate,
Safed Pool, Saki Naka, Andheri (E),
Mumbai 400 072, Maharashtra

Geetika Kambli

+91 22 2859 6358 / +91 22 2859 4394

geetika@futurefactory.in

www.futurefactory.in

SMART CIRCUIT
Intelligent real-time application of technologies.
The smart system integrates with a changing external environment, ensuring a standard purification level irrespective of the water source.

FORMAL QUALITY
Flowing sensual surfaces - Building reassurance yet attractive
The design creates a sense of reassurance, which though non-imposing, is still contemporary & attractive.

Design Company:
Future Factory

Project:
Frost-free Range of Refrigerators

Client:
Godrej & Boyce Mfg Co. Ltd
Appliance Division

Design Team:
Jashish Kambli, Milouni Kapoor, Sandesh Salaskar, Vinod Manne and Vinod Tambe

ABOUT THE PROJECT

A new range of frost-free refrigerators designed to address the 'New Face of Indian Kitchens', bringing functionality that reflects the changing needs of modern India. Sleek, fresh styling complements built-in functionality to create a user-centred and aspirational product.

KEY FEATURES

- Easy access: Quick-access flap allows easy access to frequently used foods
- Better air circulation: Through an extruded duct in translucent plastic
- Large crisper: Allows weekly stocking offering more convenience
- Sturdy and sleek: Trim-less toughened glass shelves combine sleek looks and durability

A55, Nandjyot Industrial Estate,
Safed Pool, Saki Naka, Andheri (E),
Mumbai 400 072, Maharashtra

Geetika Kambli

+91 22 2859 6358 / +91 22 2859 4394

geetika@futurefactory.in

www.futurefactory.in

ABOUT THE PROJECT

D-fine workstations give a home-office feel to its users with complete control over how they would like to use the space around them. Dfine smartly uses storages and screens to carve out spaces and avoid cubicle feel. Varied surface levels, intuitive storages, and display shelves add to Dfine's product value.

KEY FEATURES

- Configurations for individual or interactive work
- Multiple finishes for colour themes
- Power and data interference avoided
- Integrated storage for space-saving
- Adapts to varied work cultures
- Clean and simple detailing

Plant 13 Annex, Godrej & Boyce Mfg Co. Ltd, Pirojshanagar, Vikroli, Mumbai 400 079, Maharashtra

Mr E. Venkat

+91 22 6796 5656 / 5959

even@godrej.com

www.godrej.com

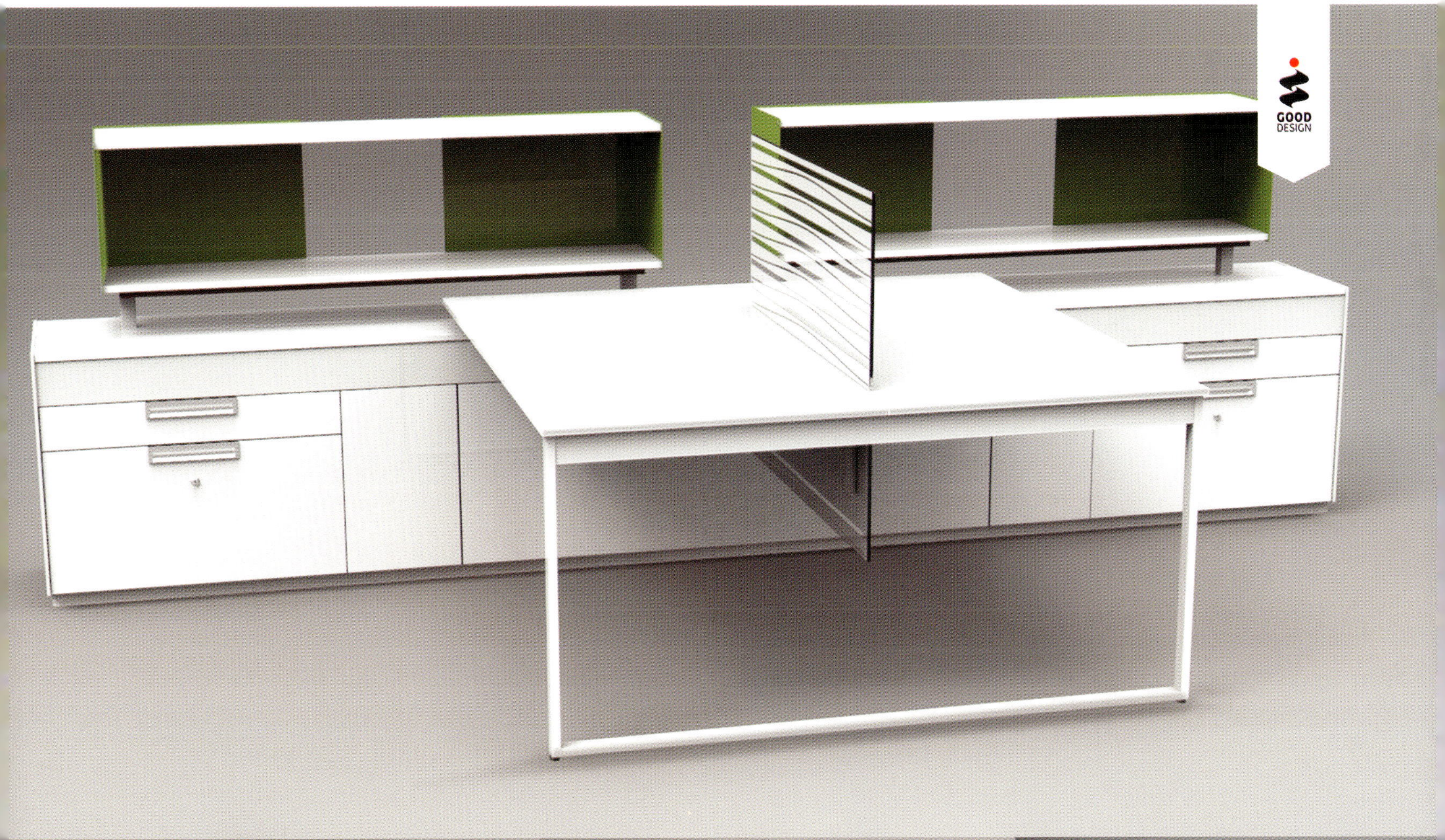

Design Firm:
Godrej Interio In-house Design

Project:
Dfine Office Furniture System

Design Team:
Lalitesh Mandrekar, Devesh Mistry, Haribabu D., Ajinkya S., Binny Dassi

GOOD DESIGN

IDI 2014

Design Firm:
Godrej Interio In-house Design

Project:
Hyacinth Bed Set

Design Team:
Jogy Abraham, Vaishali Lahoti Shah, Rupendra Amare, Shyam Thakkar

ABOUT THE PROJECT

The Hyacinth allows use in compact rooms without compromising on the utilities; a king-size bed with pull-out drawers that act as side tables; and a dresser integrated with the wardrobe. Hyacinth maximizes on the volume occupied by the bed and the wardrobe by providing storage. The Hyacinth has a unique innovation of sliding roller shutters. It provides complete and peripheral access to the storage in the bed and the wardrobe. The play of light with the transparency and opacity of the tambour brings dynamism.

KEY FEATURES

- Complete solution for compact bedrooms
- Saves 40 per cent aisle space
- Multiple utilities in two units
- Doubly secure locker
- Effortless access to storage
- Brush rails to prevent dust percolation
- Rounded edges for safety
- Knock-down and flat pack

Plant 13 Annex, Godrej & Boyce Mfg Co. Ltd, Pirojshanagar, Vikroli, Mumbai 400 079, Maharashtra

+91 22 6796 5656 / 5959

www.godrej.com

GOOD DESIGN

Design Firm:
Incubis Consultants (India) Pvt. Ltd

Project:
Lullaby — Range of affordable infant-care products

Client:
GE Healthcare India

Design Team:
S. Paldas, A. Anand, Himaka, Gunveen Ayush Jain, Palak Mittal, Amit K. Gulati, S. Rajan, Ravi Kaushik, A. Gupta, Vikram, Umasankar, S. Mehrotra, Soruban, Satish, Robin Mathew Isaac, Mohana, M. Patrimath, K. Kulkarni, B. Negi, Arvind Kumar, Anand Kumar

ABOUT THE PROJECT

GE Healthcare worked with Incubis to co-create and successfully launch three innovative 'low-cost, high-value' products for the Maternal–Infant Care segment. The aim was to design disruptive products that use the latest technologies to help reduce infant mortality. The solutions are simple, robust, extremely reliable and particularly suited for rural and similar low-resource settings.

KEY FEATURES

Lullaby Infant Warmer — Prime

- Designed from the ground-up in response to the unique realities of villages and small towns
- Only two moving parts and a super-tough reusable Kevlar probe
- Ergonomic, lightweight, compact and mobile, with large wheels to tackle uneven surfaces

Lullaby Resus Prime / Resus Plus

- Integrated solution with suction, bag & mask resuscitation, single-knob control
- Designed to reduce errors and provide rapid workflow by utilizing a single integrated device for multiple procedures, allowing users to focus on the infant rather than the equipment

259, Okhla Industrial Estate, Phase III,
New Delhi 110 020, Delhi

Mr Amit Krishn Gulati

+91 98101 17072, +91 11 4311 0500
+91 11 4311 0510

incubis@incubis.net

www.incubis.net

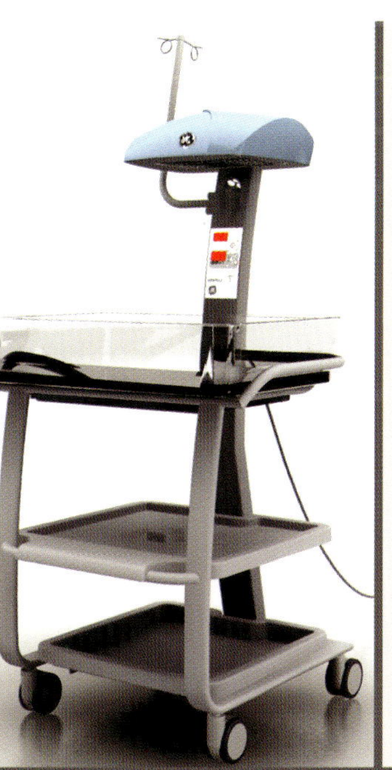

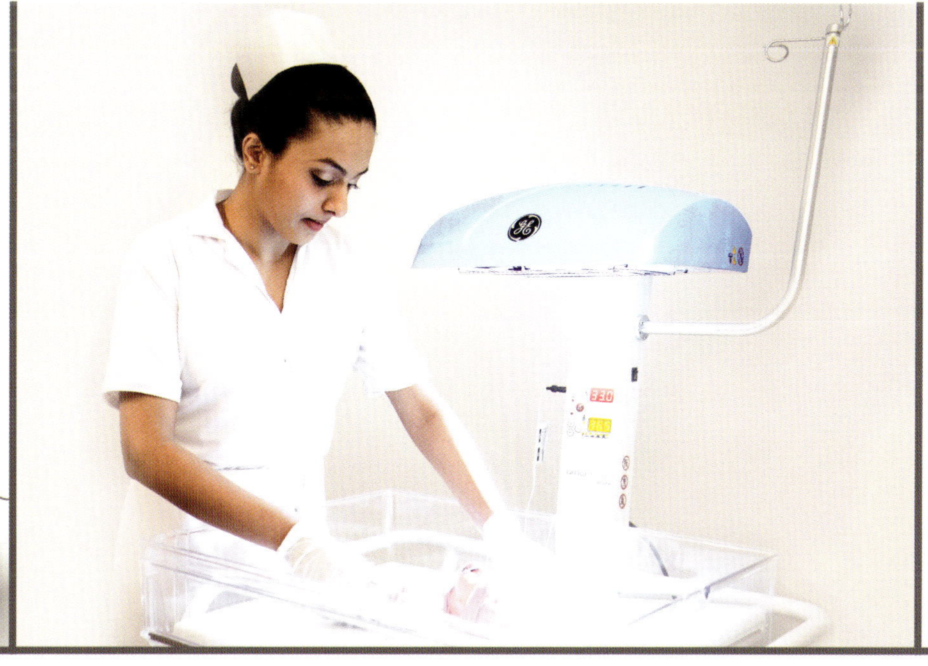

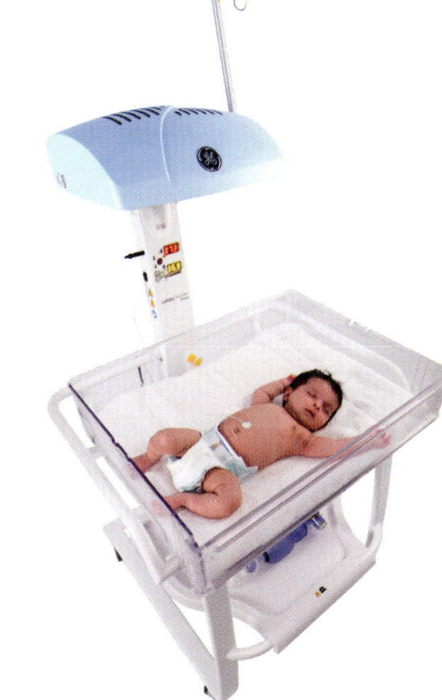

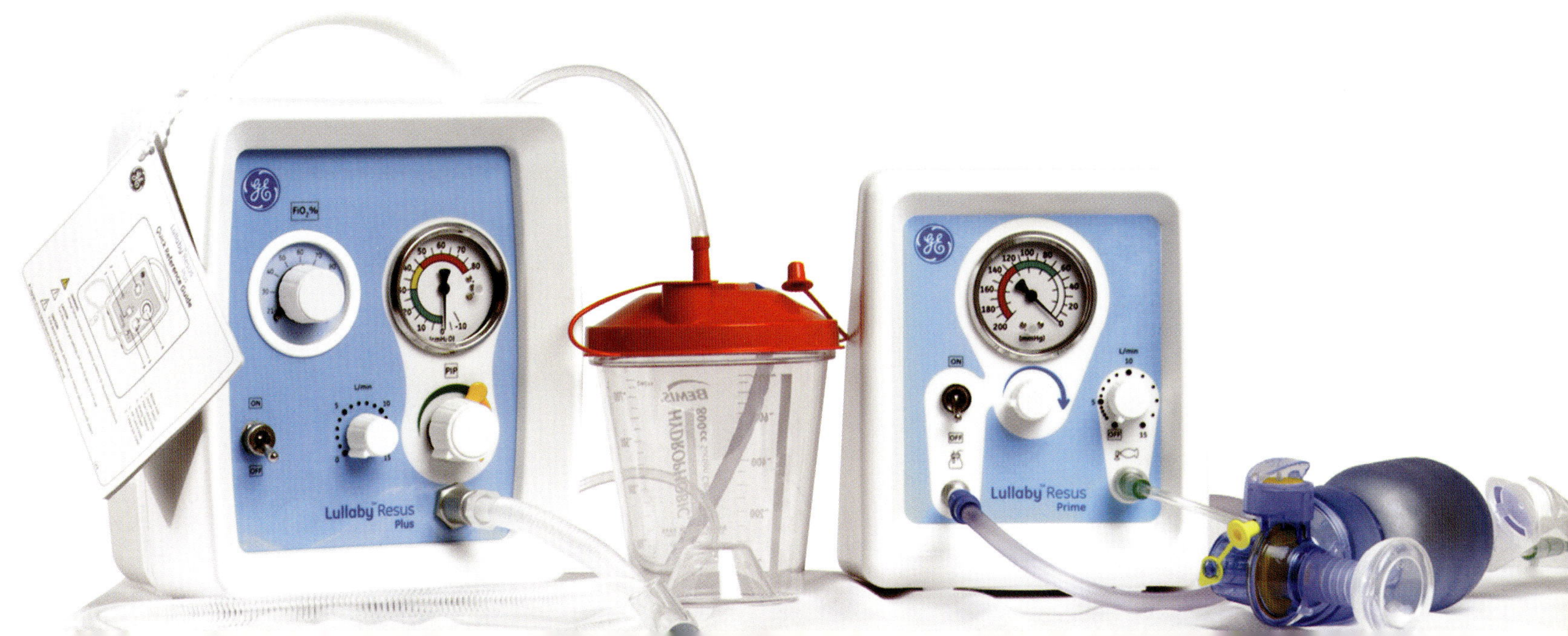

Design Firm:
Infinity Cookware & Home Appliances

Project:
Mini-Heart Mould Set

Client:
Infinity Cookware & Home Appliances

Design Team:
Narendiran Reddy Simmachalam

ABOUT THE PROJECT

The uniquely designed heart-shaped mould can be used for making muffins / cakes / cookies and Indian dishes like idli / dhoklas and orappam. This product can be used for steaming with a cooker, or baked in an oven or range. The creative heart moulds create enthusiasm among kids to have food with excitement and happiness. This innovative and creative product makes cooking a great pleasure, and eating cooked items becomes even more exciting.

KEY FEATURES

- Heart-shaped baked / steamed items like idli / muffins and cakes can be made
- Creative heart shape generates better appetite
- Easily stackable and compatible with cooker, utensils and ranges

B1, Sakthi Gardens, Phase 1,
TVS Nagar Road, Kavundampalayam,
Coimbatore 641030, Tamil Nadu

S. Kasthuri

+91 9489475036

design@infinityappliances.com

www.infinityappliances.com

Mini Heart mold set

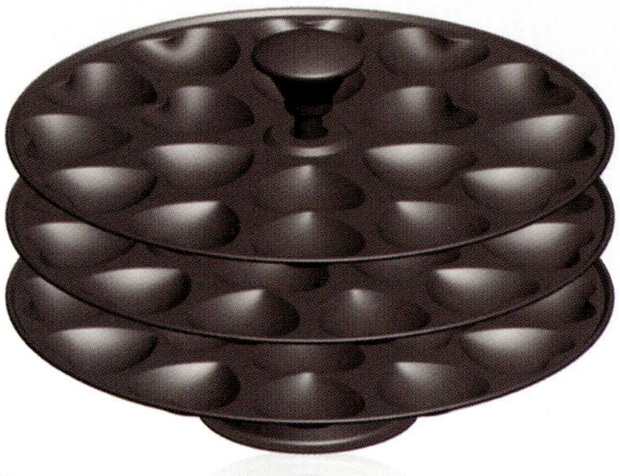

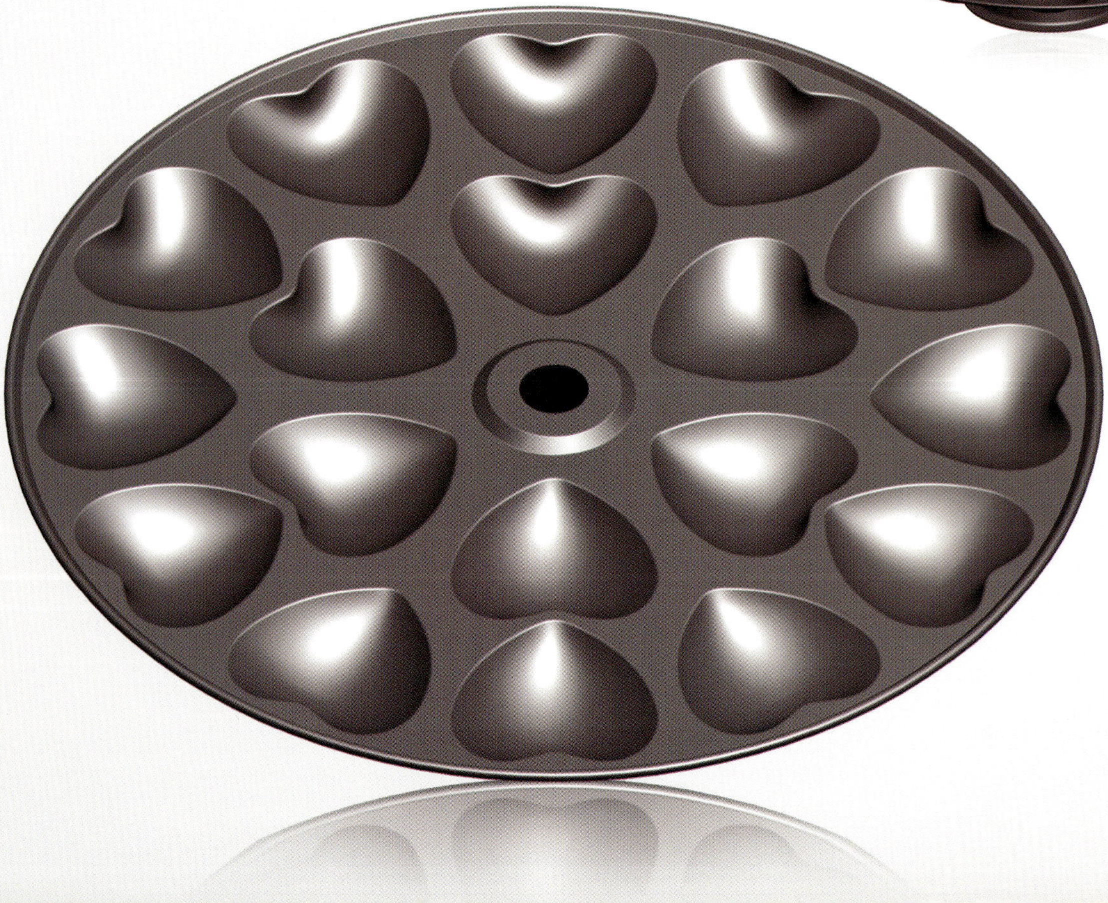

Product Usage

Can be used in stainless steel or Aluminium pressu cooker (Regulator weight should be avoided during steaming) from 6 Ltr. capacity onwards.

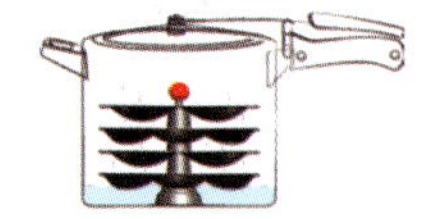

Pressure Cooker w/o regulator

Any utensil with lid that ca contain the idli set and suitable for steaming can also be used.

Cookware with closed Lid

Can be used in electric cooker too, from 1.8 Ltr onwards

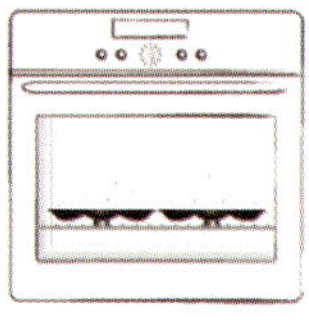

Ranges for Baking

Can be used in Ranges / Ovens for baking. Please use individual plates.

ABOUT THE PROJECT

The product is a wood-router machine which is used for making grooves, shapes and engravings on wooden pieces, with the end users being carpenters and skilled persons working in the wood industry. This machine makes complex shapes and profiles with a high-surface finish, as compared to manual operations.

Design Company:
Jagseer Singh Grewal

Project:
Wood-Router Machine
(Wood-Engraving Machine)

Client:
Joginder Electric Works

Design Team:
Jagseer Singh Grewal, Pardeep Kumar, Amritpal Singh

KEY FEATURES

- Improved aesthetics by changing body profile
- More balanced product while working, increased safety feature
- Reduction in component, thus reducing cost
- User-friendly
- Maximum use of nylon material
- Special lens for magnifying view area

#403, Ward No. 15, Dhulkot Road,
Dashmesh Nagar, Ahmedgarh,
Sangruru 148 021, Punjab

Mr Harjit Singh Aulakh

+91 16125 32049, +91 98140 30485

woodpeckerman@hotmail.com

www.indiamart.com/joginder-electricalworks/packer-man-products.html

LUMIUM

ABOUT THE PROJECT

Lumium Innovations worked collaboratively with Stovekraft to design a mass-market, low-cost mixer that can cater to the latent needs of a South Indian kitchen. Lumium followed its evolved design process to develop the mixer and its accessories, making it a success in its market segment.

Design Firm:
Lumium Innovations Pvt. Ltd

Project:
Super Storm Mixer

Client:
Stovekraft Private Limited

Design Team:
Lumium Industrial Design Team

KEY FEATURES

- Compact & contemporary design
- Wave shape for better cleanliness
- Easily accessible handles, knobs, switches
- Distinctive & ergonomic jar insert
- Excellent durability & corrosion resistance
- Zero-cracking jars
- Forced air-circulation technology (FACT)

A-504, Shapath 4, S.G. Highway,
Ahmedabad 380 051, Gujarat

Mr Rajesh Kapote

+91 76000 18879, +91 79402 05555

rajesh@lumium-engg.com
info@lumium.com

www.lumium.com

Design Firm:
Neodes

Project:
Design of Premium Digital X-ray Range

Client:
Allengers Medical Systems Limited

Design Team:
Team Neodes

ABOUT THE PROJECT

We helped an Indian X-ray manufacturer who has more than a 65 per cent market share to innovate its digital X-ray premium range to make its products truly global. Its newly developed user interface with LBD and mechanical user settings reduces the radiation exposure to patients and caretakers as well as helps in doing quick examinations. Brand-new aesthetics and newer manufacturing techniques helped them build a cost-effective yet truly international product range.

KEY FEATURES

- Radically new aesthetics platform, keeping in mind the fact that their manufacturing ecosystem gives them a considerable lead over global players
- New features which will appeal to both users & buyers and help them position their product as a value product rather than a cost-effective product
- Soft and pastel colours along with balanced bright colours gives a distinct identity
- The design has helped them create a strong bond with existing customers and opened a new regulated market
- Design helps the company to attract global leaders for collaboration

601, Niche Crown, Near Megh Malhar,
Bavdhan Khurd, Pune 411021, Maharashtra

Mr Abhijit Takale

+91 98906 27011

keepinnovating@neodes.in
abhijit@neodes.in

www.neodes.in

Make your
Product truly
Global

ABOUT THE PROJECT

Leading Biometry Company wanted to create a new range of attendance and access-control devices which would create a brand-new identity and create a platform for their range of products which shares its DNA. We created a simple, compact, elegant and technologically up-to-date aesthetics platform for their new-generation devices. The new range seamlessly adopts the formal language and shares the same DNA to create a strong impact.

KEY FEATURES

- Capacitive input keypads
- Modular architecture saves initial investment, takes care of various sensors and helps build various versions with minimum change
- Can be combined with various colours to keep up with changing needs and trends
- Universal design takes into account blind users and those less abled by resorting to voice guiding
- Designed to address industry-specific needs by offering modularity and flexibility

601, Niche Crown, Near Megh Malhar, Bavdhan Khurd, Pune 411 021, Maharashtra

Mr Abhijit Takale

+91 98906 27011

keepinnovating@neodes.in
abhijit@neodes.in

www.neodes.in

Design Firm:
Neodes

Project:
Design of Access Control Devices

Client:
Smart I Electronics Systems Pvt. Ltd

Design Team:
Team Neodes

INDIA DESIGN MARK
GOOD DESIGN
awarded in 2013

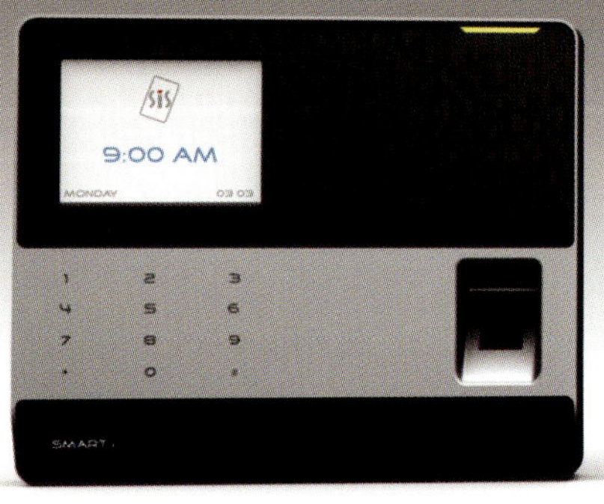

Design Firm:
Neodes

Project:
Design of Neonatal Product Range

Client:
Zeal Medical Pvt. Ltd

Design Team:
Team Neodes

ABOUT THE PROJECT

Zeal Medical is an Indian company with 20 years of rich experience in the manufacture of neonatal products. With a sincere desire to innovate their product range to create a strong leadership brand which can compete against global leaders like GE, Philips, etc, and also to differentiate them from local unorganized low-end product competition, a new product range has been introduced.

KEY FEATURES

- The innovative patent-pending temperature sensor with capacitive technology and a dual parabola heater increases infant safety and avoids potential hazards
- Soft and balanced product form evokes faith in parents and all stakeholders
- User interface design and product design makes doctors and the baby more comfortable in a demanding environment
- Hospitals and doctors profit from well-designed and engineered products. This cost-effective yet high-quality product is also affordable for the wider market

601, Niche Crown, Near Megh Malhar,
Bavdhan Khurd, Pune 411 021, Maharashtra

Mr Abhijit Takale

+91 98906 27011

keepinnovating@neodes.in
abhijit@neodes.in

www.neodes.in

MEDICAL DESIGN EXCELLENCE AWARDS

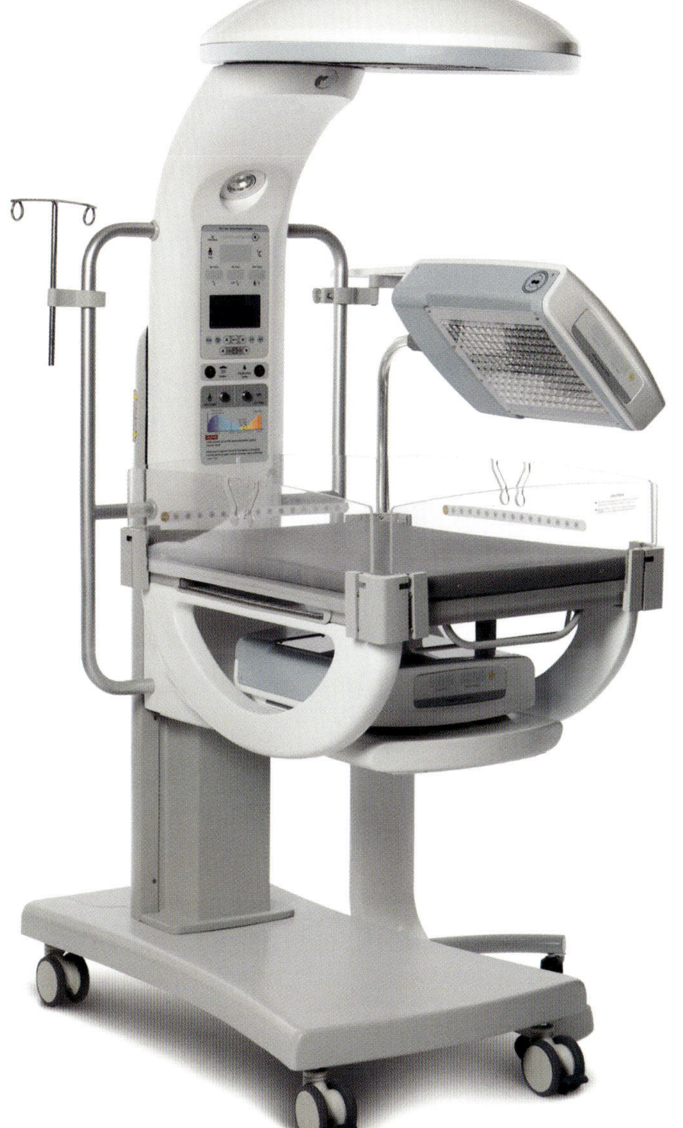

Make your Product truly Global

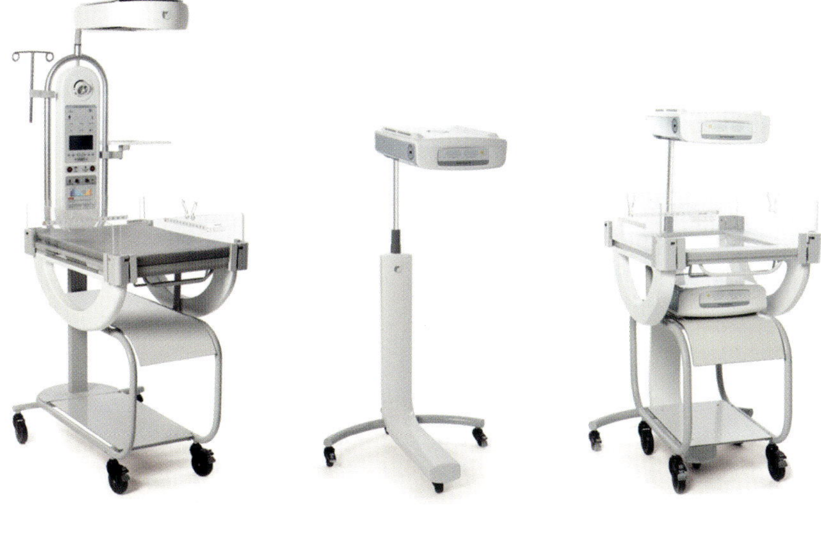

ABOUT THE PROJECT

The Side-Shift Rotavator is designed for optimum performance in the centre and offset positions. This feature enables the rotavator to work in areas where tractors have limited access due to their size, and in areas with low-hanging branches of trees. The lead screw shifting mechanism can be easily adjusted. Mainly used for tilling in vineyards, orchards and other row-crop fields.

Design Firm:
New Swan Multitech Ltd

Project:
Side-Shift Rotavator

Design Team:
Harmeet Singh, Mandeep Singh, Didar Singh, Tarlochan Singh

KEY FEATURES

- Enables one to work in smaller and limited-accessibility areas for tractors (below the low-height trees)
- Equipped with a safety cover to protect the branches from damage during the side-shift operation
- Allows flexibility to work in the centre as well as in an offset position
- Robust lead screw design with position lock and easy shifting
- Best tillage alternative for vineyards, orchards

622, Industrial Area B
Ludhiana 141 003, Punjab

Mr Barunpreet Singh

+91 161 4356084/ +91 98155 44622

barunpsingh@swanindia.com
bsa@swanindia.com

www.swanindia.com

Design Firm:
Sahajanand Technologies Pvt. Ltd

Project:
Magnus Digital — The Diamond Planning System

Design Team:
Mr Rahul Gaywala, Mr Munjal Gajjar, Mr Arjun Mavani

ABOUT THE PROJECT

Magnus Digital (a rough diamond planner) is an indispensible tool in the age of the highly competitive diamond-manufacturing process, due to its design innovation, mechatronics excellence and optical accuracy. Creating a 3D topographical model of the rough diamond, Magnus Digital allows the user to generate a 3D map of imperfections within the rough diamond, and also uses artificial intelligence to provide optimized yield.

KEY FEATURES

- 5-zone illumination for remarkable visual performance
- Smart & intuitive software UI
- HD colour digital vision system
- Pleasing visual presence
- Compact, space-saving desktop solution
- Fewer clicks for all operations
- Modular design ensures high uptime
- Intuitive workflow for steep learning curve
- Simple operation method enables high production

Sahajanand House, Parsi Street, Saiyedpura, Surat 395 003, Gujarat

Mr Rahul Gaywala

+91 26124 51451–58 / +91 99251 47373, +91 26124 27947

rahul@sahajanand.co.in

www.sahajanand.co.in

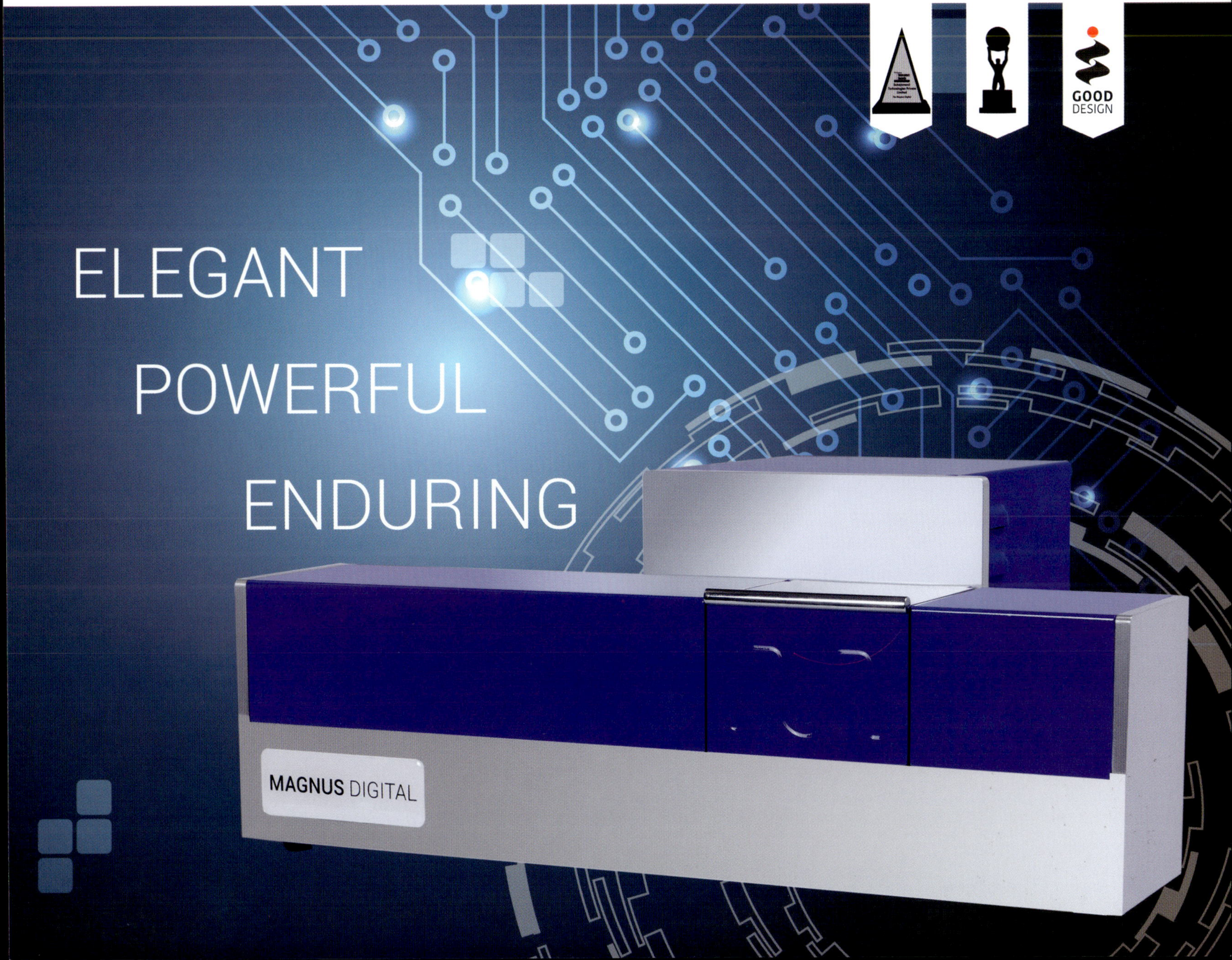

GOOD DESIGN

ELEGANT

POWERFUL

ENDURING

MAGNUS DIGITAL

Design Firm:
Studio ABD Design Services Pvt. Ltd

Project:
Money Plant (Coin Holder)

Client:
Studio ABD Design Services Pvt. Ltd

Design Team:
Abhijit Bansod, Amrita Bansod

ABOUT THE PROJECT

There is an infamous paradigm that proclaims: 'Money doesn't grow on trees.' We beg to differ. The money plant is a beautifully crafted aluminium tree that magically holds on to coins that come its way. Watch the plant grow as the coins arrange themselves all over the branches, like leaves on a tree. With this money plant, you can grow your money at home!

KEY FEATURES

- Magical experience
- Everyday organizer
- Contemporary lifestyle accessory

Lakeview Farm, Near Shell Petrol Pump,
Whitefield — Old Airport Road,
Ramagondanahalli, Bangalore 560 066
Karnataka

Ms Shipra Bhargava

+91 88842 11132, +91 80 2854 3061

shipra@studioabd.in

www.studioabd.in

ABOUT THE PROJECT

The Umaid Bhavan Queen recreates the magic and beauty of the Palm Court through the oval-shaped case with its studded bezel ring. Petit links reflect the fine craftsmanship.

KEY FEATURES

- Statements of fine living
- Contemporary luxury
- Celebrating Indian grandeur
- Harmoniously fusing the magical past with contemporary styling
- Evolved craftsmanship

Lakeview Farm, Near Shell Petrol Pump, Whitefield — Old Airport Road Ramagondanahalli, Bangalore 560 066, Karnataka

Ms Shipra Bhargava

+91 88842 11132, +91 80 2854 3061

shipra@studioabd.in

www.studioabd.in

Design Firm:
Studio ABD Design Services Pvt. Ltd

Project:
Nebula Umaid Bhavan Palace Collection

Client:
Titan Industries Ltd

Design Team:
Abhijit Bansod, Amrita Bansod

Design Firm:
Tanishq Design Studio

Project:
IVA Fine Fashion Jewellery

Client:
Titan Company Ltd, Jewellery Division

Design Team:
In-house Design Team

ABOUT THE PROJECT

IVA from Tanishq is the first serious collection to foray into fine fashion jewellery in India, where fine jewellery typically is not related to fashion trends. Changes in society as well as apparel habits influenced the target group, 'The IVA Lady', who, rather than blending in, strives to express her individuality with her sense of fashion and styling.

KEY FEATURES

- Fashion connect: Bollywood launch
- New colour-gemstones cut
- Modular jewellery
- Minimal yet feminine styling
- Affordable range of options

No. 132 / 133, Divyasree Technopolis,
Off HAL Airport Road, Yamlur Post,
Yamlur, Bengaluru 560 037, Karnataka

Chandrakala

+91 80 6660 9537

kala@titan.co.in

www.titan.co.in

NJA

STARS OF THE INDUSTRY AWARDS

Detachable stone Modular Necklace
Stone can be attached to one Ear-ring
(One spare stone provided to attach to the other ear ring)

Design Firm:
Tanishq Design Studio

Project:
MIA — Colours @ Work

Client:
Titan Company Ltd, Jewellery Division

Design Team:
Tanishq Design Studio

ABOUT THE PROJECT

Mia — Colours @ Work is conceptualized based on the need for fine workwear jewellery that is affordable and chic. An innovative philosophy of adding meaning to each colour for all days of the week has been used in this collection, like Monday Blues and Wednesday Purples.

KEY FEATURES

- Pioneering lapidary — interesting cut stones
- Unique matte & glossy-finish stones
- Colour stones characterizing each day at work
- Innovative manufacturing techniques
- Affordable range
- Contemporary & chic styling

No. 132 / 133, Divyasree Technopolis,
Off HAL Airport Road, Yamlur Post,
Yamlur, Bengaluru 560 037, Karnataka

Chandrakala

+91 80 6660 9537

kala@titan.co.in

www.titan.co.in

DESIGN OMICS AWARDS 2012

Mia presents colorful workwear designs that add a dash of color to everyday work.
An innovative philosophy of adding meaning to each color for all days of the week.
Crafted using vibrant preious stones and 14K gold, they are sure to brighten up even the most boring of jobs.

S M T W T F S

UNIVERSAL Designovation Lab

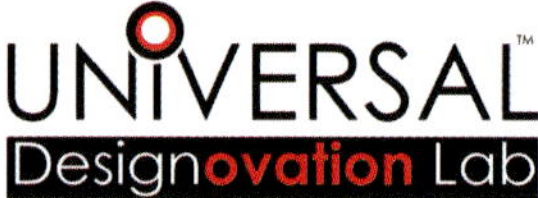

Design Firm:
Universal Designovation Lab LLP

Project:
Induction Furnaces

Client:
Magnalenz, Ahmedabad

Design Team:
Chinmay Yagnik, Bhagvanji M. Sonagra,
Bhavin R. Dabhi, Sujit Prasad,
Neha Srivastava

ABOUT THE PROJECT

Magnalenz induction furnaces are designed and produced by studying all available existing furnaces in the world, adapting all their superior features, adding all up-to-date technologies and combining the necessary needs indicated by foundrymen. Lower power consumption, enhanced-economy modern semiconductor technology and an optimum furnace design minimize the power demand and consumption, thus reducing the melting cost.

KEY FEATURES

- Design awarded the I Design Award
- Integrated capacitor bank
- Touch-based control panel

27 Ajanta Park, University Road,
Rajkot 360 005, Gujarat

Mr Bhagvanji Sonagra, Mr Bhavin Dabhi

+91 99982 54226, +91 99789 66679

universaldesignovationlab@gmail.com

www.udlab.in

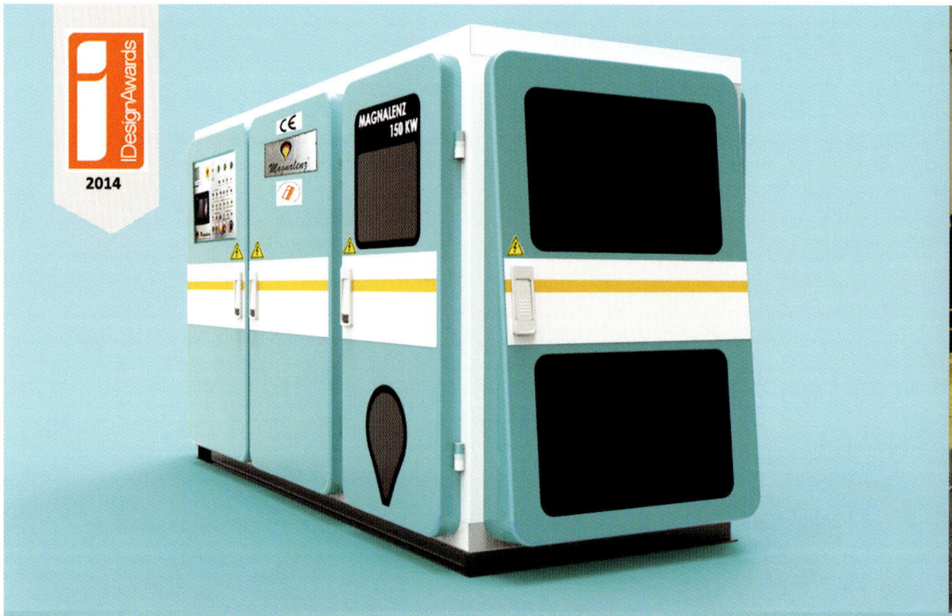

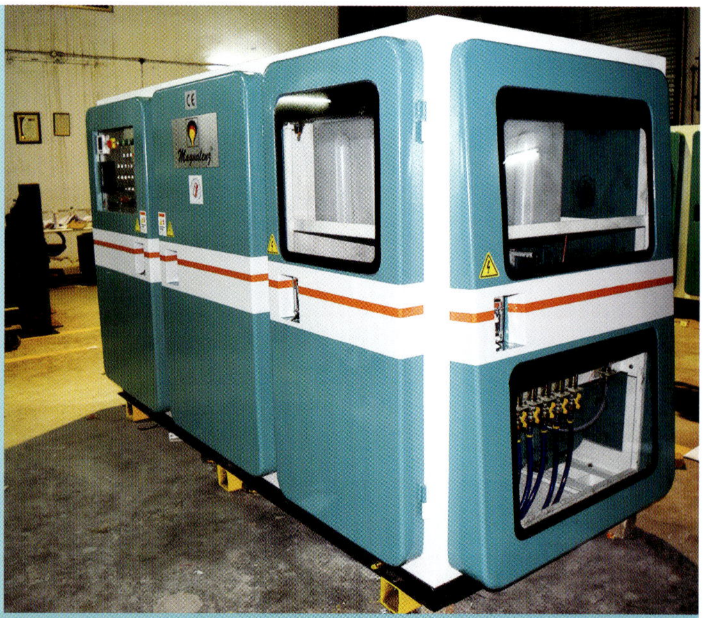

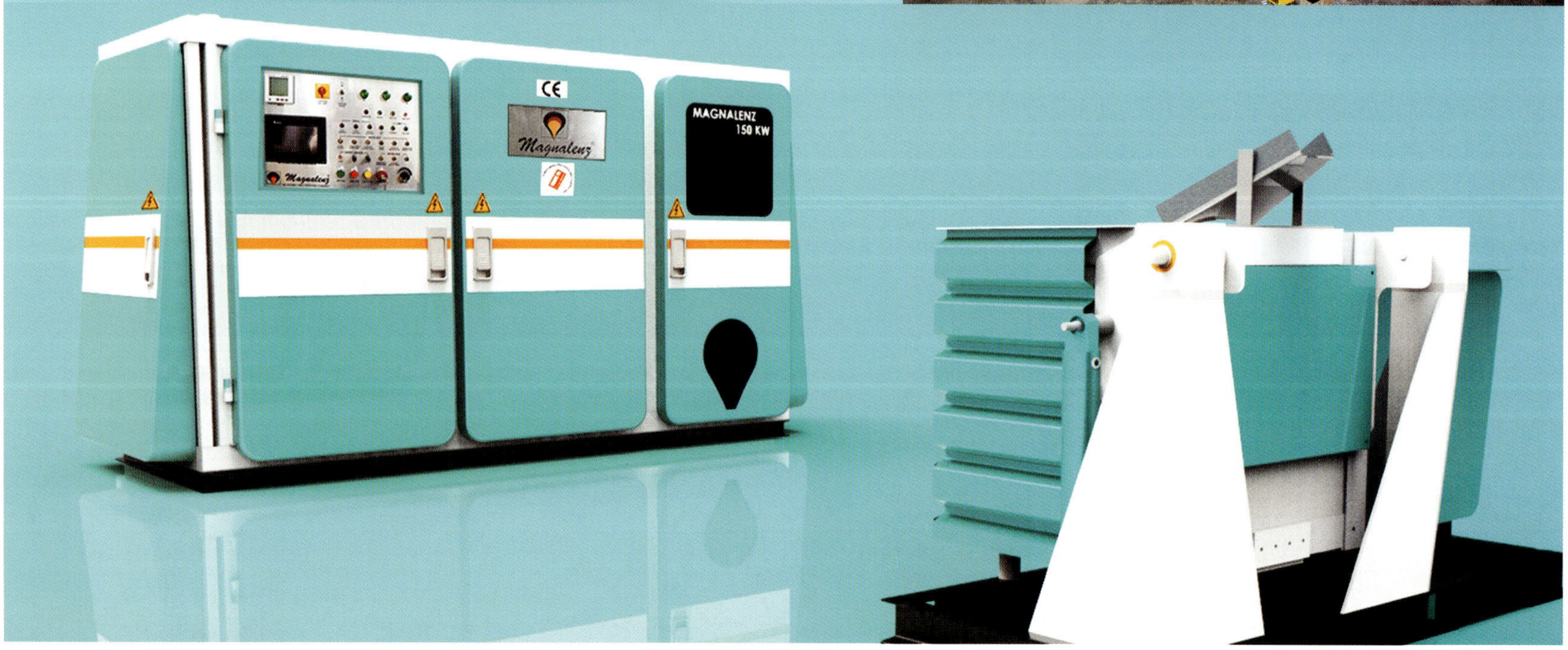

ABOUT THE PROJECT

The dual wax injection press has been designed with the dual station at a right angle, with vertical and horizontal injection nozzles at both the stations. The vertical nozzle with ejector system is a patented design and is an easy-to-operate arrangement. Only one operator is required to operate both the stations. Touchscreen-based control panel gives real-time operation cycle parameter and status for easy control.

KEY FEATURES

- I Design Award–winning design
- Dual operation station
- Patented wax mechanism
- Touch-based control panel

27 Ajanta Park, University Road,
Rajkot 360 005, Gujarat

Mr Bhagvanji Sonagra, Mr Bhavin Dabhi

+91 99982 54226, +91 99789 66679

universaldesignovationlab@gmail.com

www.udlab.in

Design Firm:
Universal Designovation Lab LLP

Project:
PMP Dual Injection Machine Press

Client:
PMP Machine Tools

Design Team:
Bhagvanji M. Sonagra, Bhavin R. Dabhi,
Amit G. Patel, Summit Patel,
Rahul Gohel, Neha Srivastava

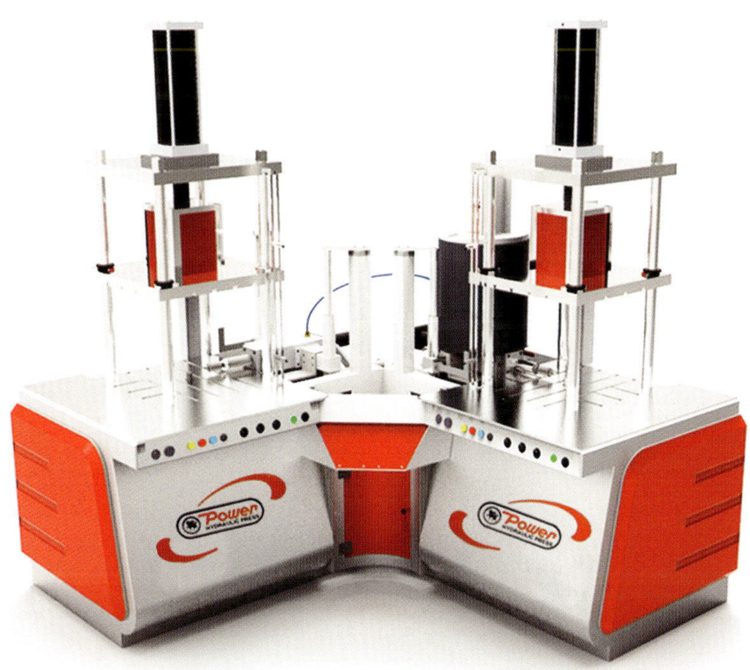

Design Firm:
Universal Designovation Lab LLP

Project:
Neonatal Phototherapy Machine

Client:
Dev Bio Care Private Limited

Design Team:
Bhagvanji Sonagra, Bhavin Dabhi, Neha Srivastava, Rahul Gohel

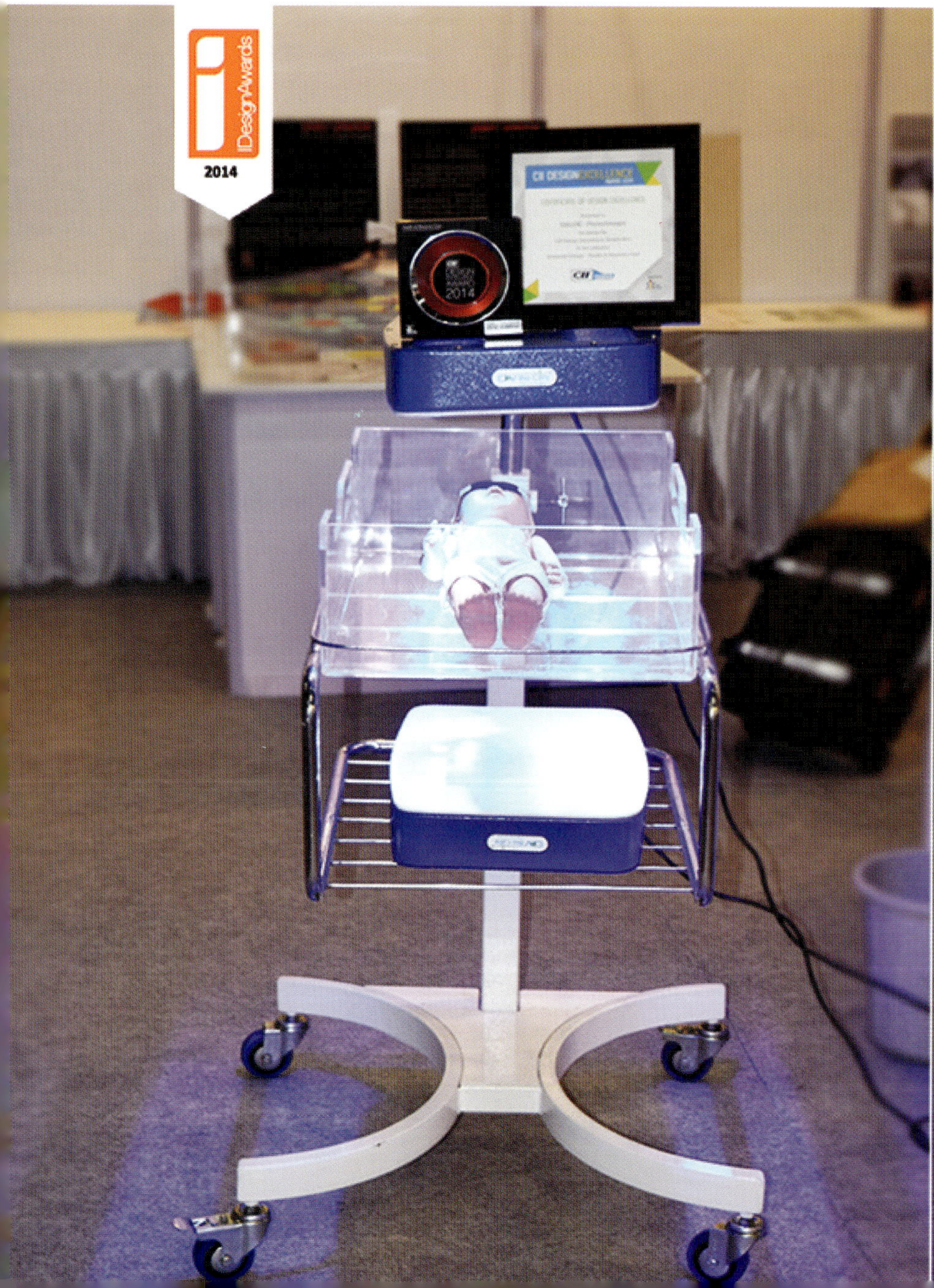

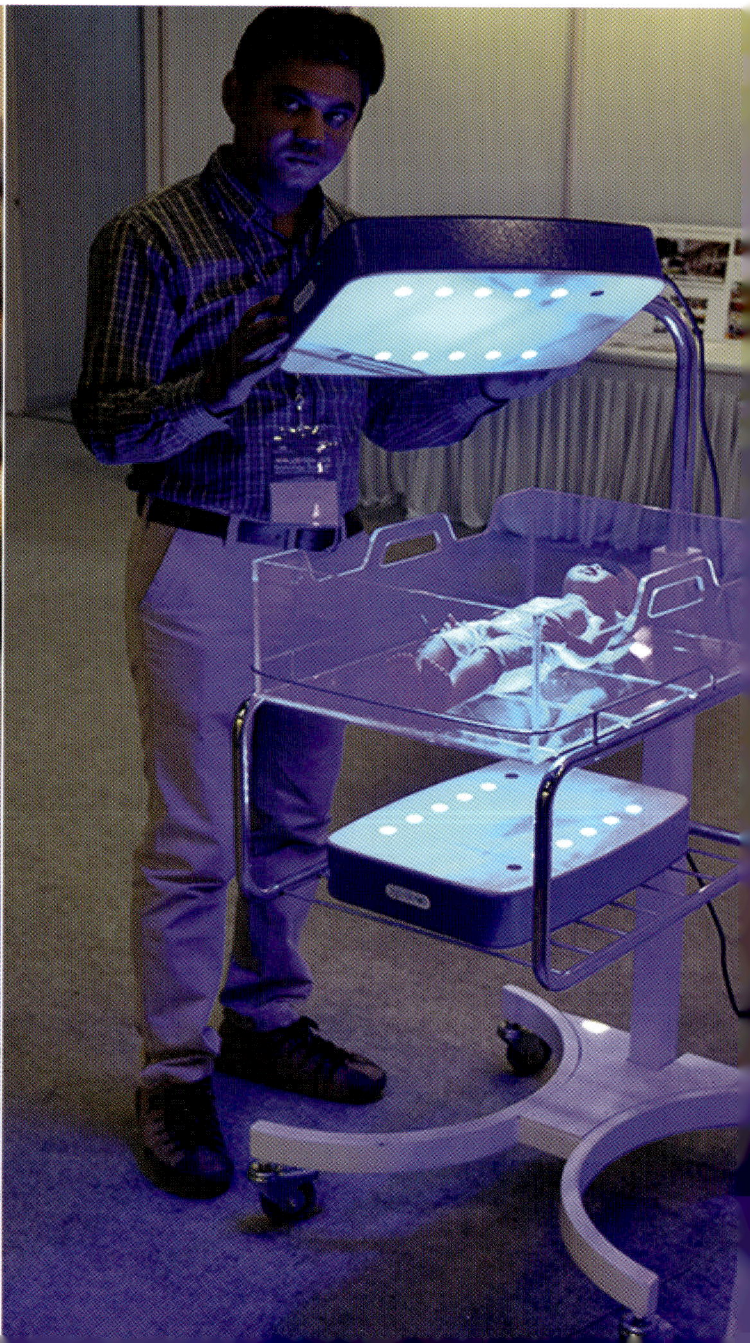

ABOUT THE PROJECT

An award-winning intensive LED phototherapy machine, modern and yet simple solution for jaundice management for newborns. This product is designed as per the Indian condition and values. This new product has flexibility as well as an effective and easy mechanism to get an accurate result every time. The detachable baby unit gives space optimization and easy to travel with.

KEY FEATURES

- Intensive jaundice management
- Phototherapy unit

27 Ajanta Park, University Road,
Rajkot 360 005, Gujarat

Mr Bhagvanji Sonagra, Mr Bhavin Dabhi

+91 99982 54226, +91 99789 66679

universaldesignovationlab@gmail.com

www.udlab.in

iDesignAwards 2014

ABOUT THE PROJECT

The Impaq-Pro laptop trolley and satchel is a business bag designed to protect the laptop from the vagaries of business travel. The smart organizer houses a tablet (iPad), cables, a mobile phone, adapters, pens, business cards and a portable hard-drive. A sleeve, thoughtfully provided to stash away the last-minute newspaper, is a delight.

KEY FEATURES

- Innovative laptop protection method
- Quick front-stow newspaper sleeve
- Single-piece elastic interior organizer
- Self-adjusting and expanding organizer

DGP House, 5th Floor, 88C,
Old Prabhadevi Road,
Mumbai 400 025, Maharashtra

Mr Vasant Dewaji

+91 22 6653 9000, +91 22 6653 9015

vasant.dewaji@vipbags.com

www.vipbags.com

Design Company:
VIP Industries Limited

Project:
Carlton Impaq Pro

Design Team:
VIP Design Studio

ABOUT THE PROJECT

Stark is a premium 4- wheeled zippered hard case available in 3 sizes, and used for long-and short-haul travel. A structured and formal form coupled with top-of-the-line functionality delivers amply to the needs of the global business traveller.

KEY FEATURES

- Two equal-packing compartments
- Centre zipper access
- Zipper-covered interior front-shell
- Separate shoe-pouch for organized packing
- Additional laundry bag
- Unique striped ridges on surface
- Lightweight yet sturdy form
- Appealing colours for the business traveller

DGP House, 5th Floor, 88C,
Old Prabhadevi Road,
Mumbai 400 025, Maharashtra

Mr Vasant Dewaji

+91 22 6653 9000, +91 22 6653 9015

vasant.dewaji@vipbags.com

www.vipbags.com

Design Company:
VIP Industries Limited

Project:
Carlton Stark

Design Team:
VIP Design Studio

ABOUT THE PROJECT

Spacelite is the lightest upright 4-wheel trolley bag from VIP. It is for the evolved traveller seeking an optimized weight-to-strength ratio, which conforms to all international and domestic airline regulations.

KEY FEATURES

- Cabin-size baggage weighs only 1.95 kg
- Ultra-lightweight construction materials and components
- Lightest ever 1.8 gm metal pullers used
- Appealing teal-blue business colour
- New soft-top look
- Strolling is smooth with 4 wheels
- Highlighted zippers and trims
- TSA lock for US travels

DGP House, 5th Floor, 88C,
Old Prabhadevi Road,
Mumbai 400 025, Maharashtra

Mr Vasant Dewaji

+91 22 6653 9000, +91 22 6653 9015

vasant.dewaji@vipbags.com

www.vipbags.com

Design Company:
VIP Industries Limited

Project:
VIP Spacelite

Design Team:
VIP Design Studio

02 2014

INTERACTION DESIGN

DESIGN STACK

Design Firm:
Design Stack

Project:
MyScreen App

Client:
MyScreen India

Design Team:
Priyanka Bhasin, Anoop Patnaik

PROJECT TITLE

My Screen — It Pays

BACKGROUND

MyScreen is a non-intrusive mobile advertising platform that enables location-based interaction between advertisers and users. Once the application is installed and activated on your smartphone, it presents offers based on the user's customized profile settings.

CHALLENGE

Design Stack had to create branding that resonated with both users and advertisers. We had to present a solution that appealed to target groups on either end of the scale: youth vs the business community, personalization vs advertising and sales.

SOLUTION

Design Stack created an award-winning branding identity that appealed to young working professionals and college students: personalized, easy, friendly, open and empowering. In-depth research and attention to detail found expression in a handwritten style in the hand symbol, depicting the hand touching the screen — a to-the-point yet youthful monogram. The simple yet highly effective tag line — It Pays — served the end user and the advertiser, with an emphasis on the obvious product benefit to both. The application UI design carried forward this approach with an intuitive interface, and quirky and fun, yet instantly recognizable widgets.

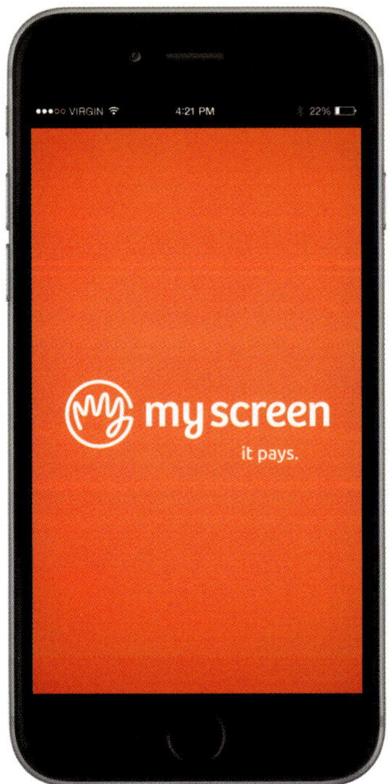

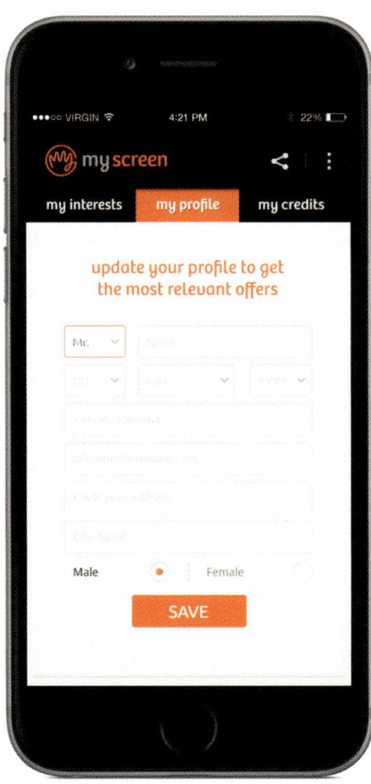

CLIENT SPEAK

Design Stack's approach and output successfully reached two disparate audiences. It actively promoted a new service and a new platform for advertisers — a novel way to serve interest-based, specific advertising to users who had consciously registered for more information and deals on particular product selections.

ABOUT THE DESIGN FIRM

Design Stack is a strategic branding and design studio. We help a wide range of businesses realize a greater awareness and demand for their offerings. Our detail-oriented approach results in effective and imaginative solutions. Design Stack is committed to making communications work harder, look better and stay on top longer.

SERVICES

- Design strategy & positioning
- Visual identity
- UI / UX design
- Advertising campaigns
- Packaging & merchandising
- Signage
- Environmental graphics
- Print communication

Flat #4, 1st Floor, Ashiyana Building,
13 N.S. Road, Juhu,
Mumbai 400 049, Maharashtra

Priyanka Bhasin, Anoop Patnaik

+91 98215 82293, +91 98199 15112

contact@designstack.com

www.designstack.com

manage your settings in a few seconds

show credits off startup screen

ad

turn off my ad display

Design Firm:
Exit Design

Project:
Outlined — Design Automation Tool

Client:
Connect Brand Marketing

Design Team:
Karn Malhotra, Vidhi Trivedi, Vinay Saini

PROJECT TITLE

A SaaS-based print design automation tool for people to express themselves in their local language.

BACKGROUND

The cloud computing market will touch $1 billion in 2015 in India, with SaaS frameworks accounting for $650 million. We wanted to create a design-focused SaaS framework that will help designers validate their value at the next level while making the creation of print collateral accessible to anyone.

CHALLENGE

How do we make global quality design available to individuals and businesses across tiers 1, 2 and 3 in India, in a format where they can do it themselves with no training and absolute control over time, cost and quality?

SOLUTION

Design is made up of a few key elements — type, colour, space, balance, image, etc. As much as there is a premium for a 'concept' — there's a huge need for just better quality design available to more people across the board that doesn't come only from a 'design studio'. Therefore, it was important to demystify the 'elements' of design and create rules of expression around their use that would be easily understandable by anyone — without having to learn them. 'Outlined' is built as a cloud-based SaaS tool; it is accessible to anyone, even on lower bandwidths, on the go, and in their local language. Democratize Design.

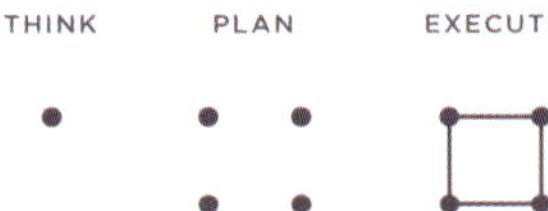

BRAND GUIDELINES

Delivery brand consistency - through and through, no matter where you are

MULTIPLE LANGUAGE

Everyone speaks more than one language - as do your customers

QUICK OPTIONS

Click a button and watch the magic of multiple options appearing

SIMPLEST WAY TO DO PRINT DESIGN ANYTIME ANYWHERE

A framework that will mean freedom from dependency on others, even if you aren't trained in the skills required for graphic design execution.

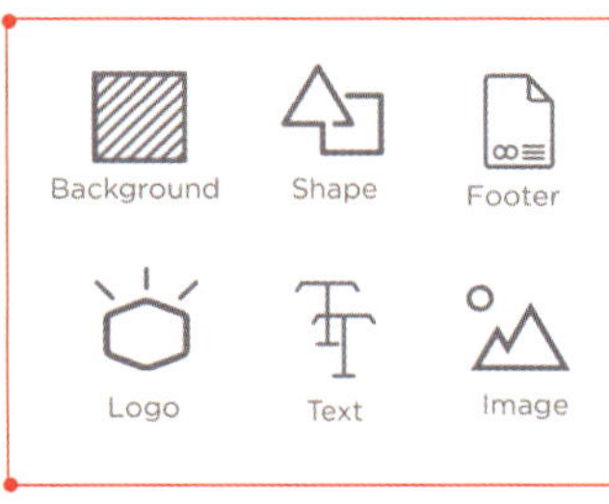

CLIENT SPEAK

"

Local-language keyboards
Brand Managers create 'Visual Briefs'
Marketing automation of brand manuals for the retail sector

ABOUT THE DESIGN FIRM

Founded in 2004, Exit Design today specializes in corporate brand manuals &UI/UX Design. Brand manuals include those for Decathlon India (sport), 3M BikeCare — ASIAPAC (Automotive) and English India Clays Limited — Thapar Group (manufacturing) amongst others. UI/UX projects include 'Uniqreate', a research automation tool for Oxford University (IDYB 2013) and websites for various corporates.

SERVICES

- Brand Manual Design
- UI/UX Design

No. 1, 2nd Floor, 3rd Main, Domlur 2nd Stage, Bangalore 560 071, Karnataka

Karn Malhotra

+91 984 552 2281, +91 80 4151 9267

karn@exitdesign.in

www.exitdesign.in

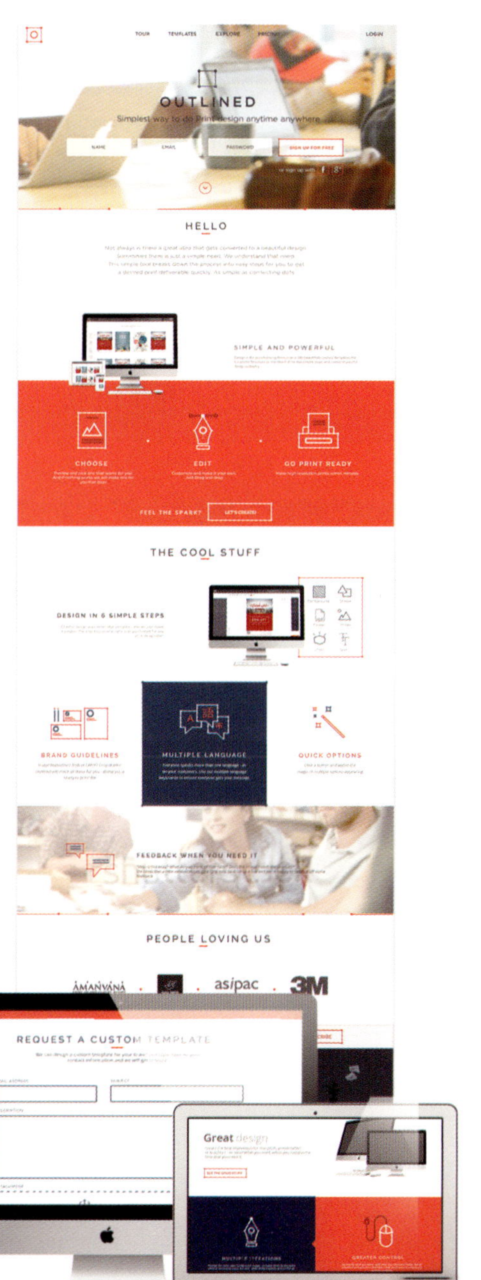

PRINTERS

Help printers deliver unexpected value and knowledge to their clients; making them as relevant today as they've always been

Make a 'creative career' path available to more at a young age, allowing them to discover and explore freely

MARKETING

Allow for marketing automation; delivering a consistent on-ground brand experience sitting in Gurgaon and activating in Trivandrum

Create original collateral yourself on a plane or in a cab; control the delivery and express what's really in your mind

Design Firm:
White Orange Works Media Pvt. Ltd

Project:
Guidezie

Client:
Cherian Sankey

Design Team:
Creative Director: Ram
Senior UI Designer: Mani
Account Manager: Varun

PROJECT TITLE

Guidezie — Online Tour Guide Booking Portal + App

BACKGROUND

The project was aimed to seamlessly bridge the gap between connecting a tourist and a local guide of any tourist place. The portal and app were to be designed including initial identity creation, tag line, UX and UI for the portal, and app on iOs and Android platforms

CHALLENGE

The project required an understanding of the entirety and the sole purpose of easily connecting a tourist to his/her preferred choice of local tourist guide when they travel across the globe. The challenge was in both the front end and back end, to seamlessly integrate the user search with a few clicks and confirm an authorized tourist guide in no time, while assuring ease of navigation, user experience and successful transaction.

SOLUTION

Design is made up of a few key elements — type, White Orange Works Media understood the complexity and nature of the requirement, and made it simpler for any user to connect to a local tourist guide, in very few steps. The identity was created such that it's quite inquisitive and attention-grabbing to its target group. Once this was achieved, the challenge of the user experience on both the web and mobile platforms were provided, wherein a user can confirm his/her tourist guide in less than 3 clicks. The UI was envisaged keeping in mind the core target group by which it would be visually enticing and yet engaging on every level of user interaction on either of the platforms.

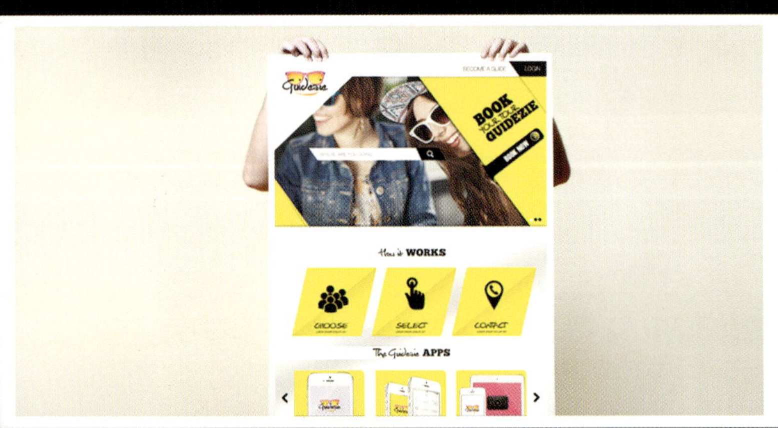

ABOUT THE DESIGN FIRM

We are White Orange Works Media, or simply, WOW Media, one of the most spoken-about communication and design agencies today. Driven by technology, our solutions and strategies are designed to give you a creative and technological edge over the competition.

SERVICES

- Corporate branding
- End-to-end web solutions
- UX & UI for web & mobile
- Digital marketing
- Strategy consulting
- Event / product launch execution
- Print & packaging designs
- E-learning

#601, 6th Floor, A Block,
Queens Corner, Opp. Indian Express,
Bangalore 560001, Karnataka

Ram: MD & Creative Director

+91 96869 77722

ram@whiteorangeworks.com
info@whiteorangeworks.com

www.whiteorangeworks.com

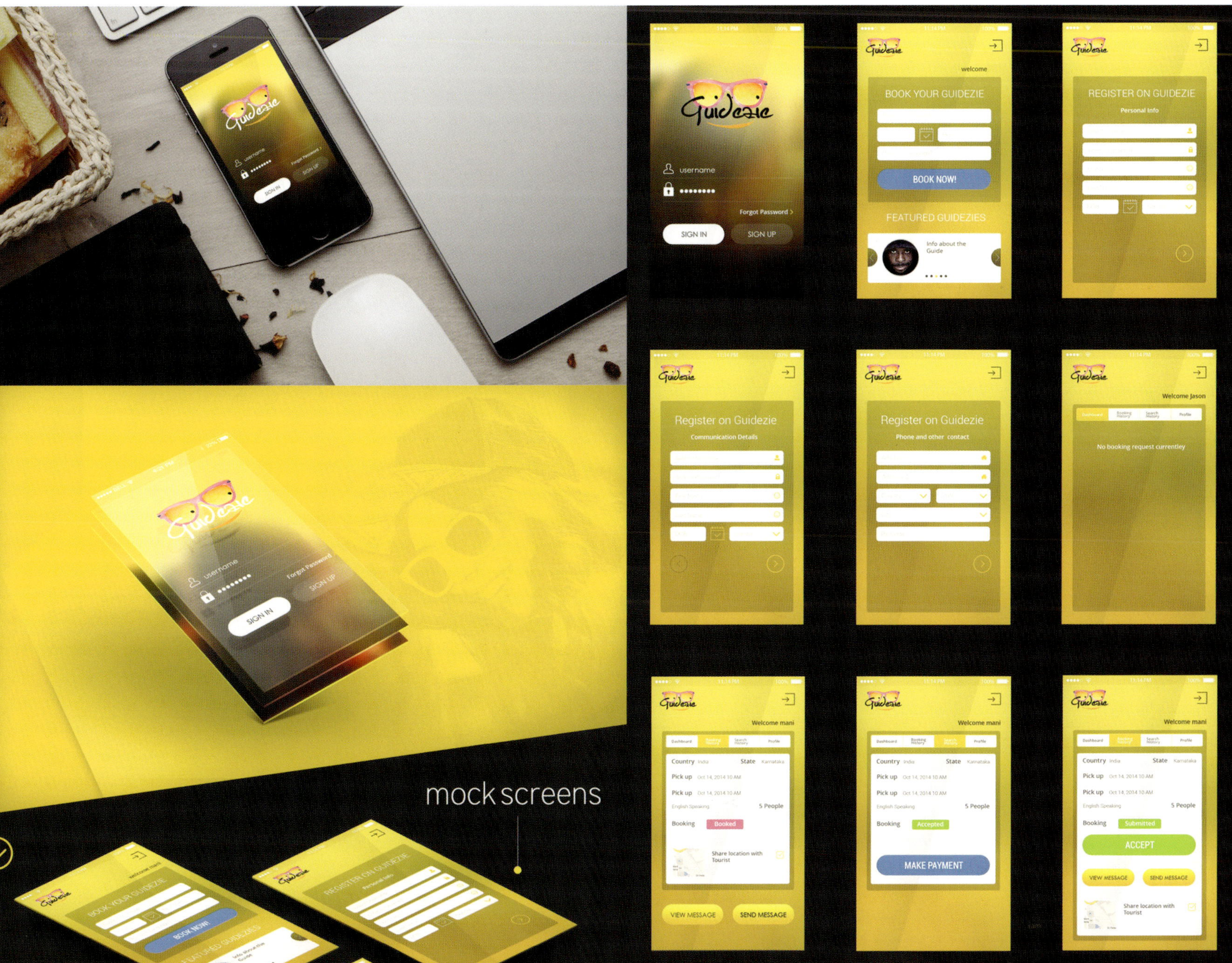

Design Firm:
Brillio Technologies

Project:
iBox

Design Team:
Brillio Design Team

ABOUT THE PROJECT

iBox — Innovation in a Box enhances field sales efficiency by demonstrating Brillio's innovative solutions and capabilities to customers in one-to-one meetings. iBox makes customer conversations more lively, insightful and, in keeping with Brillio's brand promise of the New Know How, showcases a brand-new way of selling.

KEY FEATURES

- Showcases the latest content related to Brillio's solutions from Sharepoint pages
- Showcases sales pitches and informative videos that are relevant to the current discussion
- Showcases the capability of various Brillio practices and accelerator decks
- Connect with a Brillio specialist over the phone and email while engaging in a customer conversation

58, 1st Main Road, Mini Forest, JP Nagar, 3rd Phase, Bangalore 560 078, Karnataka

Keshav Arora

+91 97384 12448, +91 80 4012 8500

keshavma@brillio.com

www.brillio.com

studiolotus™

Design Firm:
Studio Lotus

Project:
Volvo Eicher Commercial Vehicles

Client:
Volvo Eicher Commercial Vehicles Limited

Design Team:
Ankur Choksi, Arun Kullu, Pankhuri Goel, Ananya Berry, Xabrina Martinez, Tenzin Yeshi, Sanjay Kumar

ABOUT THE PROJECT

The Volvo Eicher Commercial Vehicles (VECV) corporate showcase represents the company's vision of driving modernization in commercial transportation along with showcasing their top-of-the-line production and distribution processes. The concept of the exhibition was based on the idea of 'movement' and manifested through ribbons representing the two parent companies, moving through the space.

KEY FEATURES

Enclosed within the building's grand spiral staircase is a double-helix structure made of 1500 metal rods signifying the coming together of Eicher and Volvo. The helix transforms into sinuous ribbons of Corian in the reception lobby and becomes the skin of the exhibition space centred around a moving Installation of a cut section of a truck suspended from the ceiling. VECV's story is conveyed through interactive experiences including a touch-based Corian table, video wall, touch-sensitive TV screens with headphones narrating testimonials.

F-301, First Floor, Chaudhari Prem Singh House, Lado Sarai, New Delhi 110 030, Delhi

Ankur Choksi

+ 91 11 4057 0808

info@studiolotus.in

www.studiolotus.in

●2 2014

MOBILITY
DESIGN

Mahindra

Company Name:
Mahindra and Mahindra Ltd

Project:
New-Generation Scorpio

Design Team:
Head of Design: Ananthan Ramkripa
Exterior: Anand Gawade,
Ankur Sharma, Debrup Sanyal
Interior: Anis Ahmad, Gaurav Bhatia
Colour, Material & Finish: Ashwarya Chowdhury

PROJECT TITLE

New-Generation Scorpio

BACKGROUND

Since its launch in 2002, the Scorpio has been one of the most successful SUVs in India, transforming Mahindra's image from rural-utility vehicle-maker to true-blue SUV manufacturer with urban appeal.

CHALLENGE

The challenge was to design a fresh, new look for the vehicle, transform the positioning to 'Thrill and Adventure', give a modern, sharp feel to the vehicle. On the inside, it was a different story though; whilst the exterior had been refreshed with changing times, it was the interior that has remained the same since its launch in 2002. Hence, the new interior had to be more contemporary, with higher perceived quality that fits in well with the current times.

SOLUTION

The New-Generation Scorpio is made to look very different from its earlier avatar, by virtue of a razor-sharp, aggressive modern fascia which includes the bonnet, fenders, headlamps, grill and meshes, bumper, etc. The smart-looking alloys freshen up the sides, and the new stylish chiselled tail lamps impart a techy feel alongside the new tailgate. Headlamps and tail lamps of the New-Generation Scorpio have a magical blink-and-fade effect which gives an interesting animated character to the car. Repetition of the 'trapezium' motif on different areas, for example, the grill, alloys, demister pattern, headlamp, tail lamps, instrument panel, cluster, etc., makes the overall design quite homogeneous. The interior thematic direction was to have a structure and skin treatment to an asymmetric Instrument Panel (IP) form, where surfaces and layers are wrapped over a structure, resulting in folds and chamfers making the IP volume taut. It hints at high precision and robustness at the same time.

KEY INSIGHTS

Exterior:

It's possible to dramatically alter the perception of a vehicle in spite of engineering or carry-over constraints . . . by the sheer magic of design! It's important to create a 'WOW' aesthetic, not only around the overall form and finer details, but also by considering the functional elements. The New-Generation Scorpio has a personality which can be flamboyant, aggressive, macho and techy all at the same time!

Interior:

- Lack of harmony in the old interior
- Despite so much technology packed into the old interior, it looked dated and low-tech
- Old interior scored low on perceived quality when compared to its competitors

ABOUT THE DESIGN TEAM

The design team at Mahindra and Mahindra of India is young and vibrant, with a mix of creative designers and engineers from various prestigious institutes across the world. The team works in an environment that fosters creativity, aided by an infrastructure to realize concepts.

KEY FEATURES

Exterior:

- New, aggressive, well-sculpted fascia gives a modern feel for 'thrill and adventure' positioning
- Attention to the smallest of details like grill, meshes, alloys and lamp details imparts an overall refined appearance

Interior:

- Asymmetric Instrument Panel (IP) design
- Icy-blue mood lighting to enhance the techy feel
- Geometric cubic finish with soft embossed knitted fabric to make it feel New Age progressive

Mahindra & Mahindra, Design Studio, Automotive Sector, Akruli Road, Kandivali East, Mumbai 400101, Maharashtra

Mr Anand Gawade

+91 22 2846 7533

gawade.anand@mahindra.com

www.mahindrascorpio.com

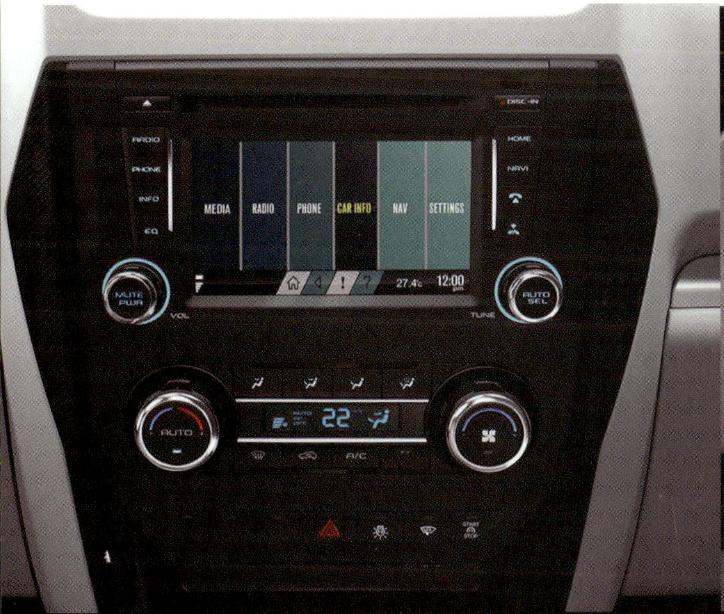

TATA MOTORS

Company Name:
TATA Motors Limited

Project:
Genx Nano

Design Team:
TATA Motors Design Team

PROJECT TITLE

Genx Nano from TATA Motors

BACKGROUND

The Genx Nano is the micro hatch from TATA Motors which comes with a host of changes and new features. 'Infinite Happiness' forms the core design philosophy of the Genx Nano.

CHALLENGE

The design of the Genx Nano is continuously evolving to match contemporary styles while retaining its distinctive timeless charm. Improved performance and enhanced utility were the key drivers for the new Nano. Combining this with the appealing aesthetics that excite the customer was the foremost objective.

SOLUTION

The smile on the Nano has now transformed into a wide grin on a confident face. The sculpted front-bumper with the humanity line, part of the TATA frontal DNA, encases the 'infinity' motif bumper grille. The new, large, circular fog-lamps complete the grinning look of the new Nano. The dark head-lamps are connected together by a black trim that proudly holds the TATA logo. The rear is all new, featuring a new bumper and an openable tailgate with an integrated tailgate spoiler.

The interiors sport new colour combinations in latte and ebony, with new paint finishes, premium fabrics and new door-trims. Embroidered 'Nano' letters and slim seat inserts in bright orange add a dash of colour to the subtle brown interiors. The new floating console with AMT shifter is convenient to operate and blends in perfectly with the new interiors.

TATA Motors Limited
Design Studio, Engineering Research Centre,
Pimpri, Pune 411 018, Maharashtra

Mr Pratap Bose

+91 20 6613 5380

pratap.bose@tatamotors.com

www.tatamotors.com

TATA MOTORS

PROJECT TITLE

Zest from TATA Motors

BACKGROUND

Following the philosophy of 'Confident Dynamism' under the DesignNext pillar of TATA Motors, the Zest is poised to be an industry leader towards design, drivability and connectivity. Possessing several industry firsts, the Zest is set to redefine the compact sedan market.

CHALLENGE

To execute a brilliant aesthetic without compromising on functionality, safety, performance and space was key. The clear purpose was to excite the customer. This was achieved with our constant endeavour to continuously evolve the design to match contemporary style and reflect a sculpture that was truly timeless.

SOLUTION

A bold and sculpted look attained by precise craftsmanship. Industry firsts including projector headlamps, LED signature daytime running lights and signature wrap-around tail lamps add to the freshness of the design.

CII DESIGN EXCELLENCE AWARDS 2014

Company Name:
TATA Motors Limited

Project:
ZEST

Design Team:
TATA Motors Design Team

CLIENT SPEAK

See who else is Zestified . . .

Autocar, India: With the Zest, Tata wants to claw back lost ground from its competitors in the crucial sub-4-metre sedan segment it first created.

Overdrive, India: I think it's time you considered walking into a TATA Motors showroom and giving the Zest an opportunity to present its case.

Top Gear: The engineers have done a stellar job, not just with the aesthetics but on technology and mechanical grounds too.

Zig Wheels: The TATA Zest marks a new chapter. It promises current design, likeable interiors, and engine and drivetrain options that should have the competition worried.

TATA Motors Limited
Design Studio, Engineering Research Centre, Pimpri, Pune 411 018, Maharashtra

Mr Pratap Bose

+91 20 6613 5380

pratap.bose@tatamotors.com

www.tatamotors.com

Company Name:
TI Cycles of India

Project:
Montra Timba

Design Team:
Sushant Jena, Raghavendra Acharya, M. Thiyagarajan, Mithun Darji, S. Ramachandran, M. Shanmugam

PROJECT TITLE

TIMBA Hybrid Series, TIM1 6061 HTAT Alloy 700X35C

BACKGROUND

Timba — Hybrid is one that blends the unique features of both road bikes and MTB bikes into a new category of bikes that are sturdy, comfortable and fast — ideal for Indian riding conditions on tarmac and pavements.

CHALLENGE

To develop a bike that delivers a superior riding experience to a first-time cyclist.

We had to create a concept infusing the unique features of MTB and road bikes into one, without compromising on comfort, control and riding efficiency.

SOLUTION

Adapt road-bike geometry aimed at high speed and acceleration in tune with MTB control and ergonomics.

MTB transmission components fused with comfort road-bike frame to give a light and efficient bike with gear ratios to handle landscapes from a city to a highway. Comfort, weight, stiffness, control — these four factors are the cornerstones of cycling efficiency. Each one is vital on its own, but more important than any individual factor is striking a balance between all of these competing elements, bringing out the maximum benefits of each attribute in such a way that no one element dominates the others. When all of these elements are balanced, when the bike disappears beneath you and simply becomes an extension of your body, that's the truest expression of efficiency.

KEY INSIGHTS

"

Indian riders seek the attributes of a high-performance bike without compromising on comfort, control and ease of ride. Timba comes with stem-pivot position located behind the front axle, providing the bike with control at slow speed and improved weight-distribution on the bike. Indian urban riding conditions lead to dirt accumulation on the bike frame, which is difficult to clean with open cables. Timba's frame features the internal cable routing. This is more than just an aesthetic choice, as the cables will be protected from the elements, allowing the bike to perform better in all conditions and also being easy to clean.
A lot of vibrations get transferred to rider's palm, causing discomfort while riding. Timba is equipped with a rigid fork which is able to dampen the road vibration through a countervail fork rake angle.

ABOUT THE DESIGN TEAM

The design team at TI Cycles of India is young and vibrant, with a mix of creative designers and engineers from various prestigious institutes across the country. The team works in an environment that fosters creativity, aided by an infrastructure to realize concepts.

KEY FEATURES

- A low step-through frame, with an upright riding position, ergonomic handlebar grips, semi-slick city tyres and stable geometry gives the control, safety and comfort you need for cycling.
- 6061 HTAT Alloy Frame for optimal stiffness-to-weight ratio packaged with AFT (Advanced Forming Technique) for stiff, lightweight, stylish, stable and performance-orientated geometry.
- 8-speed cassette hub technology, Acera Transmission for quick gear-shift efficiency.

Post Bag No. 5, C.T.H Road, Ambattur,
Chennai 600 053, Tamil Nadu

Mr Sushant Jena

+91 44 4209 3450
+91 87544 24084

sushantjena@tii.murugappa.com

www.montra.in
www.bsahercules.com

CII DESIGN EXCELLENCE AWARDS 2014

Design Firm:
Godrej & Boyce Mfg Co. Ltd

Project:
Godrej 1.6 Tonne 3-Wheel Electric Counterbalance Forklift Truck

Client:
Godrej Material Handling

Design Team:
Mr Rahul Jadhav & Mrs Swapnali Joshi

ABOUT THE PROJECT

Godrej 1.6 Tonne 3-Wheel Electric Counterbalance Forklift Truck is a compact material-handling equipment powered by clean sources of energy; it is designed to work in constrained workspaces with state-of-the-art technology, features and a high level of operator comfort for efficient handling of material. The product is designed to operate with long service intervals due to its inherent robustness.

KEY FEATURES

- High visibility
- Joystick control with armrest
- Anti-rollback system
- Electro-hydraulic steering
- Low-effort battery rollout system
- High level of operator comfort
- 90 per cent recyclable

Godrej Material Handling, Plant 16,
Pirojshanagar, Vikhroli (E),
Mumbai 400 079, Maharashtra

Mr Sameer Chandekar

+91 22 6796 4660, 1800 225 454

mhemktg@godrej.com

www.godrejmhe.in

1.6 Tonne 3 Wheel
Electric Forklift

Made in INDIA
Made for WORLD

Optimal Utilization of Space
- with compact design & tight turning radius

High Productivity
- with best in-class performance parameters

Advanced Safety & Low Maintenance
- with wet disc brakes

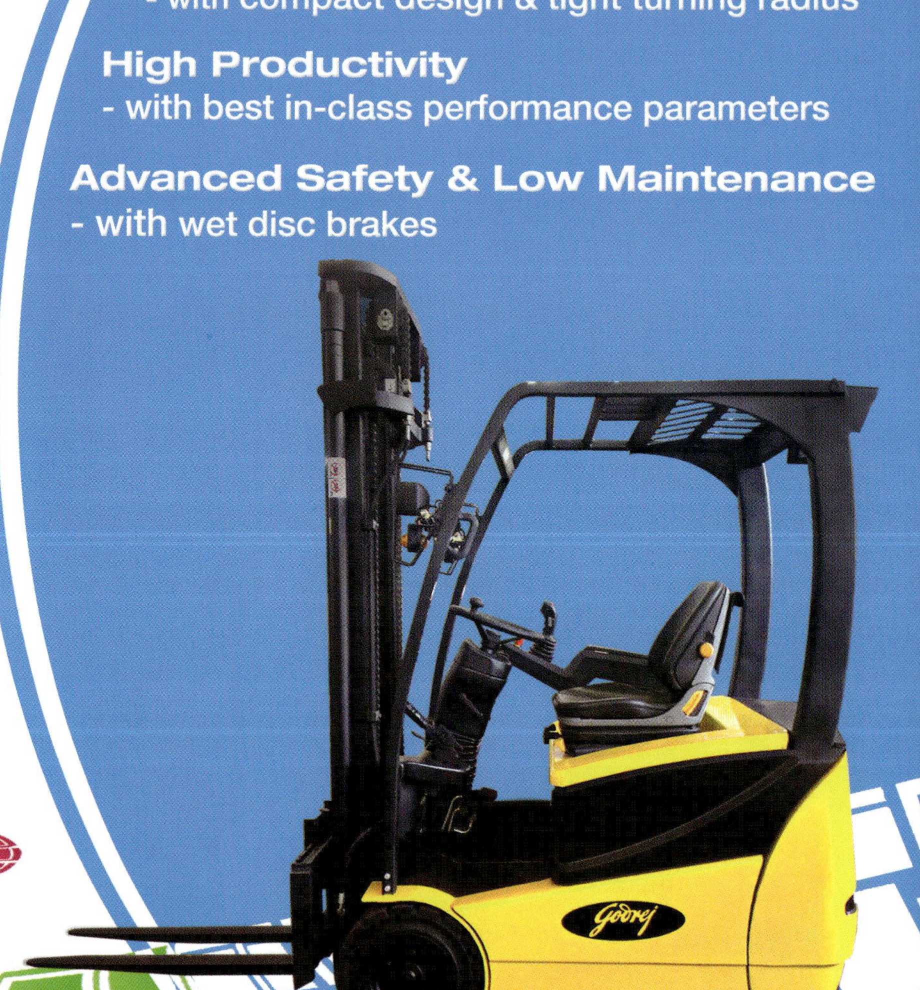

TATA MOTORS

EXCELLENCE AWARDS 2014

Company Name:
TATA Motors Limited

Project:
TATA ULTRA

Design Team:
In-house Design Team

ABOUT THE PROJECT

The TATA ULTRA is the new-generation, segment-defining, Light Commercial Vehicle offering from TATA Motors. It sports a modern, sophisticated exterior design with high-quality details and classic, robust truck proportions.

The driver-centric interiors provide a professional, calm and comfortable operating environment with superlative ergonomics, ensuring endless hours of fatigue-free operation.

KEY FEATURES

- Modern exterior design
- Refined, comfortable interiors
- High-performance exterior lighting
- Maximum interior utility
- Multi-information driver display

TATA Motors Limited, Design Studio, Engineering Research Centre, Pimpri, Pune 411 018, Maharashtra

Pratap Bose

+91 20 661 3 5380

pratap.bose@tatamotors.com

www.tatamotors.com

●2 2014

VISUAL COMMUNICATION

DESIGN **STACK**

Design Firm:
Design Stack

Project:
Asian Paints Edutones

Client:
Asian Paints

Design Team:
Priyanka Bhasin, Anoop Patnaik, Damayanti Chakravarty

PROJECT TITLE

Transforming Learning Environments with Asian Paints Edutones

BACKGROUND

Edutones specifically targets educators and learning environments. We wanted to help educators use colour effectively, combining aesthetics and functionality to create a positive atmosphere that aids learning.

CHALLENGE

Our goal was to get educators to think about colour, to get them to see how colour influences how we connect to and navigate our world. We had to do this in a clear, elegant and engaging way.

SOLUTION

An intensive search for insights followed extensive research to see how colour, traversing age, gender and experience, directly impacts creativity, efficiency, health, morale, emotions, behaviour and performance. The physics of colour, its relationship with light, and its varying impact on different age groups and physical spaces gave birth to specially curated themes and moods. The Edutones' guide to transforming learning environments was structured to present to educators a complete solution from information about colour to fresh ideas on how colour might be combined, to steps on how to get started.

CLIENT SPEAK

Asian Paints has worked with Design Stack across brands for many years. In this period, they have contributed to our overall strategy through the development of focused marketing communications for our varied target groups. Edutones is one of the books they have designed in the recent past. It has been well received and appreciated amongst the audience.

Vijay Prakash, Asian Paints

From naming, brand-positioning, information architecture and the creation of content to colour palettes, combinations and graphics, Design Stack's strategic approach found resonance in every aspect of the process: presenting content in an intuitive, meaningful, visually exciting and actionable way. The final output is a guide and tool that offers the opportunity to create an environment that fosters learning for life.

ABOUT THE DESIGN FIRM

Design Stack is a strategic branding and design studio. We help a wide range of businesses realize a greater awareness and demand for their offerings. Our detail-oriented approach results in effective and imaginative solutions. Design Stack is committed to making communications work harder, look better and stay on top for longer.

SERVICES

- Design strategy & positioning
- Visual identity
- UI / UX design
- Advertising campaigns
- Packaging & merchandising
- Signage
- Environmental graphics
- Print communication

Flat #4, 1st Floor, Ashiyana Building
13 N.S. Road, Juhu
Mumbai 400049, Maharashtra

Priyanka Bhasin, Anoop Patnaik

+91 98215 82293, +91 98199 15112

contact@designstack.com

www.designstack.com

Design Firm:
Lemon Design Pvt. Ltd

Project:
Dandi Kutir Musium, Mahatma Mandir

Client:
Government of Gujarat
Shapoorji Pallonji Engineering and Construction

Design Team:
Lemon Design Team

PROJECT TITLE

Dandi Kutir Musium, Mahatma Mandir

BACKGROUND

Dandi Kutir aims at being a state-of-the-art tribute to M.K. Gandhi, the father of our nation. Gandhiji's vision and legacy is at the core of the Dandi Kutir Museum — a unique architectural and experiential edifice providing visitors a forward-looking space to contemplate Gandhian principles and reflect on our singular and collective futures.

CHALLENGE

The museum being based on a personality who is the father of our nation and one of the most-known leaders in world history, an authentic, unbiased yet unique portrayal of him was very critical. Not letting the extensive use of technologies overpower the content, limited availability of authentic data, and the time in which the project needed to be completed also were major challenges

SOLUTION

The museum aims at initiating the visitor on a journey that inspires oneself to seek our own answers and to master ourselves through a narrative that shifts between Gandhi's self-exploration, self-critique and his public life of struggle, closely linking his individual thoughts to universal values. Gandhi's timeless 'Experiments with Truth' is shown through a prism of his life's events in a rich, multilayered experience using innovative exhibits and immersive multimedia, visitors are transported to his world to observe, interact and reflect on the relevance of his principles today. A seamless journey through the use of physical, virtual and technological techniques of storytelling was introduced, where the visitor would move from a tactile, physical exhibit to a virtual one, set in an interpretive and sometimes realistic environment with complete ease. As the museum caters to all kinds of visitors, the communication was simplified by the use of AV media and technology, and they are guided through the whole museum narrative with the use of multilingual audio-guides.

CLIENT SPEAK

Lemon Design were the exhibit designers for our client — the Government of Gujarat's museum project at the Mahatma Mandir complex. From the very beginning, the Lemon Design team showed an in-depth understanding of the subject matter and the client's requirements. Although the subject matter was nuanced, Lemon Design demonstrated patience, great work ethic and an ability to listen to our clients during challenging times, constantly helping us when required. They worked very closely with our other consulting associates as a team to deliver a coherent design solution, and we were assured that having Lemon Design on our side, our response would always be proactive and involved. We have also been very impressed their ability to work with budgets and their valiant client service. We would not hesitate to recommend them to another client and wish them the best of luck for their future.

ABOUT THE DESIGN FIRM

Lemon Design is a strategic branding and integrated design consultancy based in Pune, India.
We use design thinking and user-centric insights to create a positive strategic difference for brands, spaces, user interfaces, retail, packaging and products.

SERVICES

- Strategic branding and identity design
- Communication design
- Spatial and experience design
- Product design
- Web/UI-UX design
- Packaging design
- Signage and way-finding
- Motion graphics and films

102 Serene Manor, Serene Estate,
Next to Vespa Showroom, Kondhwa Road,
Pune 411 048, Maharashtra

Dipendra S. Baoni
Wasim Khan

+91 98220 33742, +91 98221 95102
+91 20 6478 2278

info@lemondesign.co.in

www.lemondesign.co.in

Design Firm:
Lemon Design Pvt. Ltd

Project:
V Resorts — Rebranding

Client:
V Resorts

Design Team:
Dipendra Singh Baoni, Varun Manoharan, Athul Parameshwaran, Manosij Sarkar

PROJECT TITLE

V Resorts

BACKGROUND

V Resorts is a chain of over 15 boutique resorts across northern India, located in beautiful, scenic but remote locations.

CHALLENGE

To rebrand V Resorts with the new vision — to highlight the uniqueness of the each resort and design space and experience for longer stays and to unwind with creative leisure activities.

SOLUTION

We created a dynamic identity system, with each logo being different for each location & touchpoint, and differentiated the experience to display the uniqueness of each resort — however, the services were standardized and scalable and made consistent across properties to help brand users enjoy a seamless and predictable experience of the properties and make sourcing of livery for the brand easier across all their properties. We also helped create a strong brand message, 'Get Lost', to encourage a niche and discerning audience who could connect with the offering and wouldn't mind the extra mile to reach these resorts — and definitely to discourage the sporadic weekend tourist who would walk in purely due to lack of vacancy elsewhere.

TYPE

PHOTOGRAPHIC

TYPE
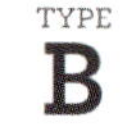
ILLUSTRATIVE

TYPE

TYPOGRAPHIC

TYPE

PICTOGRAPHIC

TYPE
E
DIRECTIONAL

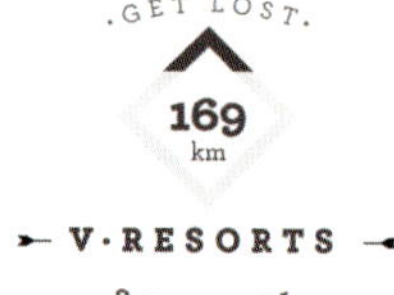

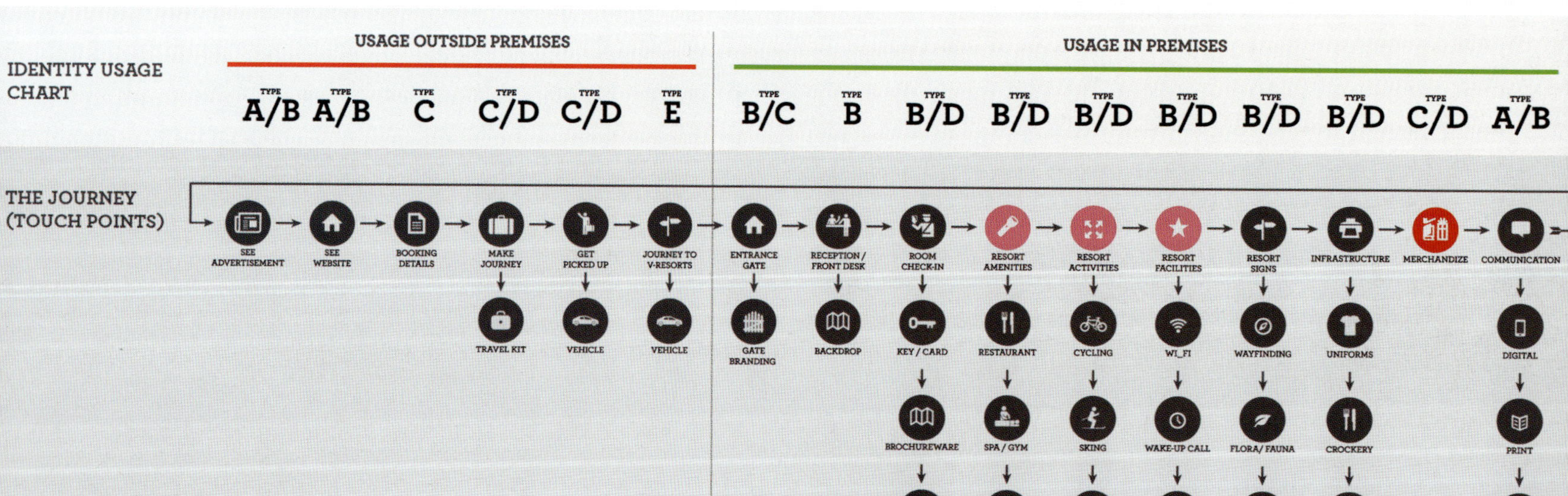

CLIENT SPEAK

I've had the pleasure of working with the Lemon team for 8 years now, across projects for Pinstorm clients, projects for my Seedfund investees and my personal investee companies. What I like is the team's approach to creativity within a tight brief. It's not predictable or boring design, and its not wild and woolly senseless creativity. It's brief-focused creativity. I wish there were more design firms like this.

Mahesh Murthy

ABOUT THE DESIGN FIRM

Lemon Design is a strategic branding and integrated design consultancy based in Pune, India.
We use design thinking and user-centric insights to create a positive strategic difference for brands, spaces, user interfaces, retail, packaging and products.

SERVICES

- Strategic branding and identity design
- Communication design
- Spatial and experience design
- Product design
- Web/UI-UX design
- Packaging design
- Signage and way-finding
- Motion graphics and films

102 Serene Manor, Serene Estate,
Next to Vespa Showroom, Kondhwa Road,
Pune 411 048, Maharashtra

Dipendra S. Baoni
Wasim Khan

+91 98220 33742; +91 98221 95102
+91 20 6478 2278

info@lemondesign.co.in

www.lemondesign.co.in

Design Firm:
The Neon Project

Project:
Gold Seal Indus Valley™
Premium Basmati Rice Branding

Client:
Hindustan Unilever Limited

Design Team:
Prashant Shingade, Vijay Rajbhar

PROJECT TITLE

Gold Seal Indus Valley™ Premium Basmati Rice Rebranding

BACKGROUND

Gold Seal Indus Valley™ (GSIV), a successful premium Basmati brand from Hindustan Unilever Limited, was first launched in the GCC countries in 1986. The product stood strong as a premium offering, rooted in its Indian origin and superior taste, and had a long-term vision of launching in India.

CHALLENGE

Even with product superiority, the overall brand mix wasn't aligned to its future vision. The brand name is quite a mouthful; the term 'Indus' that stands at the core of it proved to be unfamiliar to a majority of Indian homemakers. The rebranding challenge was to develop a credible story, simplify its essence to cut through the influx of brands in the Indian market.

SOLUTION

Our initial customer interactions confirmed that the connotation of the word 'Indus' (Latin for Sindhu) was uncommon knowledge. The unavailability of the brand in India until then also seemed to cause a level of mistrust about its history.

These insights led us to the formation of a key brand promise — the 'authentic taste of heritage'. A realistic, uniquely crafted ancient gold seal was devised as a brand mark and visual hook, proved as a mark of virtue, heritage and authenticity. The new packaging design effectively enabled GSIV to be seen as a time-tested, sought-after brand catering to the modern audience. Besides this, essential storytelling elements were carefully created, assessed and applied across all forms of communication.

BEFORE

CLIENT SPEAK

"It's a super example of how packaging alone can change the whole brand mix; super job, Neon team!

Jesal Mehta, Brand Manager

ABOUT THE DESIGN FIRM

We are specialists, generalists, left brainers, right brainers, consumers, marketers, inquirers, inventors, dreamers, realists, micro, macro, analytical, anomalous, driven by common sense and fascinated by uncommon ideas.

We believe that the best designs deliver — creatively and commercially. We possess an acumen and accountability arising out of years of experience. And we are on a mission to illuminate your business.

SERVICES

- Brand identity and experience
- Packaging and retail design solutions
- Brand language and image design
- Publication design

402, Jewel Heights, Plot 19A,
Sector 10, Kharghar,
Navi Mumbai 410 210, Maharashtra

Prashant S. Shingade

+91 98336 67764, +91 98199 73978

prashant@theneonproject.in

www.theneonproject.in

Design Firm:
Tricycle

Project:
Made for Love

Client:
Scratchgard

Design Team:
Urvi Bole, Samyadeep De, Ankita Dalvi

PROJECT TITLE

Brand Rejuvenation: Visual Language, Packaging Design, Internal Communication, Retail Activation, Brand Campaign & Brand Portal Design

BACKGROUND

Scratchgard pioneered the device-surface protection industry and enjoyed a wide market share, thanks to its strong trade network. But over a period of time, competition, in the form of duplicates and copycats, was soon scratching at the door, and our market share plateaued.

CHALLENGE

To make a mark again, Scratchgard needed to excite the market, starting with the trade network. But in this immensely low-involvement category, the regular wouldn't work. And this time around, Scratchgard needed to connect with consumers in a meaningful way.

SOLUTION

Something bold, something disruptive was needed. So we broke the mould of the category (which is primarily tech-spec-based) and took a customer-centric approach instead. We identified the core reason as to why anyone would buy a surface protector. It was simple: We are all in a relationship with our gadgets. And so emerges the new brand mantra — Made for Love. The branding approach used illustrations of real-life characters from all walks of life, all in love with their devices. This distinct brand language solved the issue of distinction and duplication; it also elicited a higher involvement with all stakeholders.

KEY INSIGHT

"The challenge was realizing there is no specific customer to talk to. Everybody has a phone/device, and we are all in a deep relationship with our gadgets today. We love our gadgets and hence want to protect them — this was the key insight, the common proposition that binds all the different personalities of the users together. Scratchgard, Made for Love.

ABOUT THE DESIGN FIRM

Tricycle is a strategic brand consultancy. Our strength lies in our unconventional way of thinking. Everything we do is strategically rooted and flawlessly executed. We help brands create value and help customers to buy into it. As your brand partner, you can depend on us to deliver on time, every time.

SERVICES

- Brand / Communication / Marketing strategy
- Brand design / Rebranding / Brand revitalization
- Corporate / Brand identity design
- Communication design / Advertising
- Packaging design / POS design
- Environment / Space design
- Website / App design
- Digital / Social design

Bund Garden Road,
Pune 411006, Maharashtra

Yuvraaj Oberoi

+91 90499 94630

yuvraaj@tricycle.co.in

www.tricycle.co.in

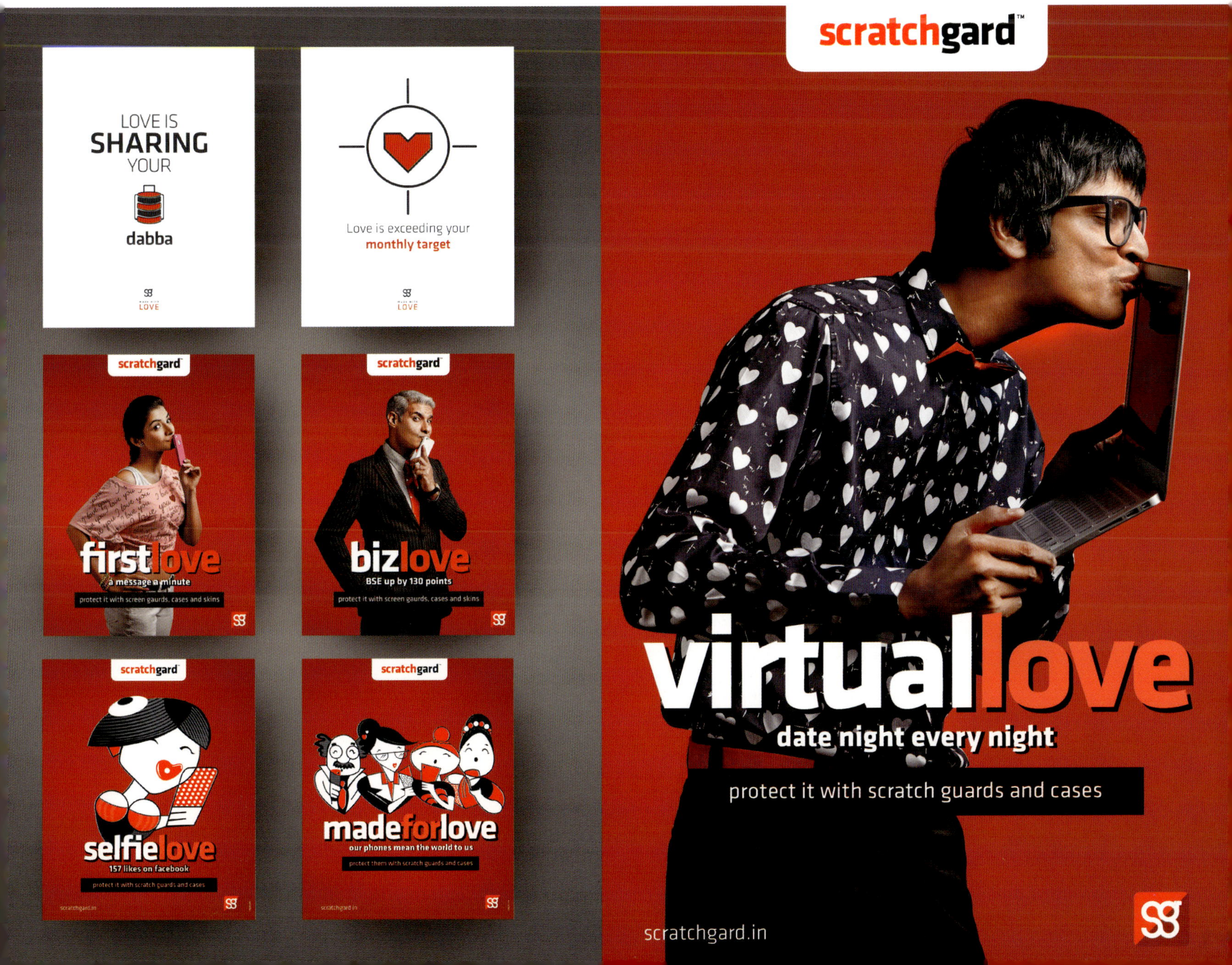
LOVE IS
SHARING
YOUR
dabba
LOVE
Love is exceeding your
monthly target
LOVE
scratchgard
firstlove
a message a minute
protect it with screen gaurds, cases and skins
scratchgard
bizlove
BSE up by 130 points
protect it with screen gaurds, cases and skins
scratchgard
selfielove
157 likes on facebook
protect it with scratch guards and cases
scratchgard
madeforlove
our phones mean the world to us
protect them with scratch guards and cases
scratchgard™
virtuallove
date night every night
protect it with scratch guards and cases
scratchgard.in

CII
DESIGN EXCELLENCE AWARDS
2014

Design Firm:
Codesign Brand Consultant Pvt. Ltd

Project:
Design for engagement:
Asian Paints — Colour Quotient magazine

Client:
Asian Paints

Design Team:
Rajesh Dahiya, Mohor Ray,
Shreeya Kurien, Siddharth Nair

ABOUT THE PROJECT

To engage with professional consumers, Codesign worked with Asian Paints to bring Colour Quotient — a quarterly colour magazine for architects and interior designers. Through the engagement, Codesign created a strong content-driven strategy to enhance the readers' experience of the brand, as a knowledge leader for colour in India.

KEY FEATURES

- Consumer engagement through content
- Enhancing brand image to colour authority
- Offers specialized colour knowledge
- Content relevant to design in India
- Contextual promotion for products
- India-focus in projects & practitioners
- Strong tool for marketing efforts

Block C2, Plot 4, Ground Floor,
Sushant Lok 1, Gurgaon 122009

Rajesh Dahiya, Mohor Ray

+91 124 4262535

solutions@codesign.in

www.codesign.in

" a creative multidisciplinary design studio for brand development & interior spaces "

Design Firm:
Cogwheel Studios™

Project:
Signage and Way-Finding Systems

Client:
MVJ College of Engineering

Design Team:
In-house Multidisciplinary Team of Designers

ABOUT THE PROJECT

The objective of the project was to simplify a 3 lakh sqft, complex building into various distinguishable zones, and clearly aid a user to travel from Point A to Point B in the minimum time. The most referred terminologies were precisely communicated via establishing effective hierarchy of information across the design solutions. The proposed design intervention also strategically distinguished the various internal zones and levels through numerical and colour codes for effective navigation, irrespective of last-minute change of classrooms and seminars within the campus.

KEY FEATURES

- Enhanced visibility
- Readability from a long distance
- Information architecture
- Ease of communication
- Scalability to address massive built-up area
- Value proposition
- Ease of manufacturing & application
- Negligible maintenance due to less/nil hardware

No. 23, First Floor, RMS Colony,
Sanjaynagar, Bangalore,
Karnataka 560 094

Krishna Mohan B.R.

080 2341 9991, +91 80503 00044

info@cwspost.com

www.cogwheelstudios.com

AREA SIGNAGE • INTERNAL ROOMS

DIRECTIONAL SIGNAGE • DROP DOWNS

KEY NAVIGATION PLANS • TOTEMS

AREA SIGNAGE • WASHROOMS

AREA SIGNAGE • ADMINISTRATIVE ZONE

AREA SIGNAGE • INTERNAL ROOMS

AREA SIGNAGE • INTERNAL ROOMS

DIRECTIONAL SIGNAGE • LIFT LOBBY

DIRECTIONAL SIGNAGE • LIFT LOBBY

design factory india

Design Firm:
Design Factory India with Fabrique

Project:
City Branding, Agra

Client:
UP Tourism

Design Team:
Sourabh Gupta, Siddharth Bathla, Jeroen Van Erp, Jari Versteegen, Robin Kemme, Mohd Masood Khan, Prashasti Chandra, Anshika Bhandari, Harnehmat Kaur

ABOUT THE PROJECT

The challenge was to give an identity to the identity of India: Agra, the city of the Taj Mahal.
To mix international expertise with contextual thinking, the Design Factory India team collaborated with Fabrique from Netherlands. The exercise was not only to give a visual identity but to design the vision and a holistic city strategy with the desired aims of the future. The designs were developed to communicate this vision to various stakeholders.

KEY FEATURES

The logo was derived from 'A':

- A is the first and last letter of the word Agra — symbolizing the glorious past and envisioned future come closer to achieve the vision
- We use the letter A as a visual device that undoubtedly stands for Agra
- 'A' is always the start of a story, therefore, we combine it with attributes that characterize and epitomize Agra; for example: A promise, A romance, A mystery
- As we say: It all starts with an A. The first letter of the alphabet. The sign of the winner, the best in class!

C 28 C, Sector 8,
Noida 201301
Uttar Pradesh

Mr Siddharth Bathla

+91 120 4640300, +91 87501 19375

mail@designfactoryindia.org

designfactoryindia.org

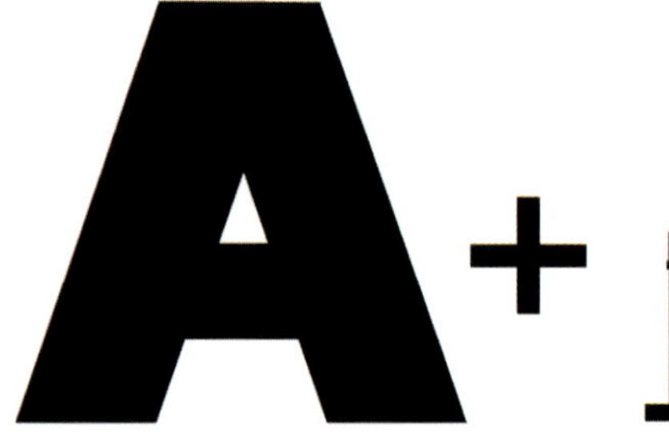

EK TYPE

Design Firm:
EK TYPE

Project:
Ek Mukta

Client:
Google

Design Team:
Girish Dalvi, Yashodeep Gholap, Noopur Datye, Sarang Kulkarni, Maithili Shingre and others

ABOUT THE PROJECT

Ek Mukta is a Unicode-compliant, versatile, contemporary, humanist, mono-linear typeface available in seven weights, which supports the Devanagari and Latin scripts. This type family is a free, licensed version of the Ek multi-script family, an ongoing project to develop a unified type family for each Indian script. The goal is to build one harmonious family across all Indian scripts without letting the visual features of one script dominate over the others.

KEY FEATURES

- Unicode-compliant
- Available in 7 weights
- Works for both print & screen
- Supports both Latin & Devanagari
- Supports Vedic signs
- In open-source; available on Google Fonts
- Extensive OpenType features
- Stylistic alternates, ligatures and fractions

004/5, Yashodham CHS, J.P. Road,
4 Bungalow, Andheri (W),
Mumbai 400 053

Sarang Kulkarni

+91 8203 47788, +91 98690 53956

info@ektype.in

www.ektype.in

एक मुक्त / Ek Mukta

एक्स्ट्रा लाईट Extra Light

लाईट Light

रेग्युलर Regular

मीडियम Medium

सेमीबोल्ड Semi Bold

बोल्ड Bold

एक्स्ट्राबोल्ड Extra Bold

'वे अनेक भाषाएँ जानते हैं!'

पृथिव्यां त्रीणि रत्नानि जलमन्नं सुभाषितम्। मूढैः पाषाणखण्डेषु रत्नसंज्ञा विधीयते॥

EQUAL

counter

अगला स्टेशन दादर, Next station Dadar

प्रथम क्र.

ANGREZI IS INDIGENOUS TO INDIA

मला होते जाणीव – एक क्षणभर, मी नाही अनेकांतील एकमेव!
तर आहे अनेकांतील एक, सर्वांतील, सर्वांचा, सर्वांसाठी – कुसुमाग्रज

eliminate the mundane

Design Firm:
EuMo

Project:
Leon's World

Client:
Rustomjee

Design Team:
EuMo multidisciplinary team

ABOUT THE PROJECT

Leon's World at Rustomjee Elanza provides a unique learning environment that fosters maximum growth and aids in the overall development of children. It is developed on the concept of multiple intelligences. Activities are designed to be child-led, with minimal or no instructions. The learning is expected to be triggered through play and curiosity.

KEY FEATURES

- Environments
- Spatial
- Conceptual interiors
- Environment branding
- Graphics

24-B, Sagar Sangeet, 58 Colaba Road,
Mumbai 400 005, Maharashtra

Gary Grewal

+91 22 4089 1919

inquire@eurekamoment.in

www.eumo.in

Conceptual Spaces
LEON'S WORLD
FOR RUSTOMJEE

Leon's World at Rustomjee Elanza provides a unique learning environment that fosters maximum growth and aids in the overall development of children. It is developed on the concept of multiple intelligences. Activities are designed to be child-led with minimal or no instructions. The learning is expected to be triggered through play and curiosity.

DESIGNOMICS AWARDS 2014

eliminate the mundane

Design Firm:
EuMo

Project:
Kohima Camp, Nagaland

Client:
TUTC — The Ultimate Travelling Camp

Design Team:
EuMo Multidisciplinary Team

ABOUT THE PROJECT

EuMo is consulting for the unique concept of 'glamping' with our client, TUTC, 'The Ultimate Travelling Camp'. TUTC develops luxury camps in India, traversing exotic locales and a calendar of seasons and festivals. This nomadic super-luxury camp introduces the discerning traveller to glamorous camping in carefully selected exceptional locations in mountains, deserts, jungles and the unexplored countryside. The tent furniture has also been developed and fabricated by our furniture company, OBLIQ.

KEY FEATURES

- Hospitality
- Luxury
- Spatial
- Master-planning
- Furniture
- Environments

24-B, Sagar Sangeet, 58 Colaba Road,
Mumbai 400 005, Maharashtra

Gary Grewal

+91 22 4089 1919

inquire@eurekamoment.in

www.eumo.in

Hospitality Design
TUTC - THE ULTIMATE TRAVELLING CAMP

A first for luxury "Glamping" in India, EuMo was involved in the design and planning of the camps and fabrication of all furniture through our furniture company OBLIQ.

foleydesigns

Design Firm:
Foley Designs Pvt. Ltd

Project:
Titan EyePlus

Client:
Titan

Design Team:
In-house Environment Design & Graphic Design Team

ABOUT THE PROJECT

Titan EyePlus is a leading eyewear brand. The new brand identity is carefully adapted into the space in order to keep the seriousness of the industry intact, while making the experience seamless and refreshing. The display system is designed to celebrate the product aesthetics and strengths. The design facilitates customer-product interaction, hence enabling a smooth buying experience.

KEY FEATURES

- Seamless and refreshing
- Designed to celebrate the product aesthetics
- Facilitates customer-product interaction
- Addressed staff-working dynamics
- Smooth buying experience

Yolee — No. 14, 202, Second Floor, Pottery Road, Richards Town, Bangalore 560 005, Karnataka

Mr Nigel Foley

+91 97409 55774, +91 80415 40181 / 82

info@foleydesigns.com

www.foleydesigns.com

foleydesigns

Design Firm:
Foley Designs Pvt. Ltd

Project:
ISH — Jaquar Stall Design

Client:
Jaquar

Design Team:
In-house Environment Design Team

ABOUT THE PROJECT

ISH is the world's leading trade fair for the bathroom experience, building services and renewable energies — that cover all aspects of future-oriented building solutions. The visitor's journey was scripted to infuse the idea of fold-unfold — the further you go, the better you explore. The space was envisaged as a flower folding into the ultimate centre. The phenomenon was accentuated with fluid forms and hints of the brand colour as elements of surprise.

KEY FEATURES

- Envisaged as a flower
- Accentuated with fluid forms
- Brand colour as elements of surprise
- Low-height ends of curves
- Enhances emotions connected with bathing

Yolee — No. 14, 202, Second Floor,
Pottery Road, Richards Town,
Bangalore 560 005, Karnataka

Mr Nigel Foley

+91 97409 55774, +91 80415 40181 / 82

info@foleydesigns.com

www.foleydesigns.com

Design Firm:
Four Dimensions Retail Design (India) Pvt. Ltd

Project:
Kethini (Premier Footwear Store)

Client:
Good Leather Shoes Pvt. Ltd

Design Team:
4D Team

ABOUT THE PROJECT

Premium Italian leather fashion in a chic, opulent environment is the signature of the new Kethini footwear boutique. The environment created from a palette of crafted leather, rich wood, marble and glass is complemented with a cozy and warm lighting concept. Stylized imagery in presentation help embellish the unique store experience.

KEY FEATURES

- Design concept inspired by Italian impressions
- Double-height, cladded facade creates a grand sense of arrival
- Differentiated by innovative display of products for personalized service
- Combination of various textures and finishes adds opulence
- Boutique-kind-of-lighting approach complements the store image
- Visual merchandising and interior environment graphics add premium finesse

No. 15, 1st floor, Saraswathi Complex,
5th Cross, Malleswaram,
Bangalore 560 003, Karnataka

Mr Nagaraja, Mr Shyam Sunder

+91 97310 09069, +91 99000 37350

enquiry@4dimensions.co.in

www.4dimensions.co.in

ABOUT THE PROJECT

Cool and funky kitsch comes to life in vibrant, coloured forms in the eclectic signature store design of the Chumbak flagship. The visual treat extends from the storefront's giant animated bubblehead into the store in the exciting, coloured interior, with iconic props and stunning visual merchandising creating an unforgettable store experience.

KEY FEATURES

- A 'Happy Place' for Chumbak enthusiasts
- Colour palette and graphic celebrate the love for India and travel
- Interesting combination of materials and forms create an eclectic look
- VM installations crafted from reused damaged merchandise
- Special lighting concept used to draw attention to design features

No. 15, 1st floor, Saraswathi Complex,
5th Cross, Malleswaram,
Bangalore 560 003, Karnataka

Mr Nagaraja, Mr Shyam Sunder

+91 97310 09069, +91 99000 37350

enquiry@4dimensions.co.in

www.4dimensions.co.in

Design Firm:
Four Dimensions Retail Design (India) Pvt. Ltd

Project:
Chumbak (Home Improvement Store)

Client:
Chumbak Design Pvt. Ltd

Design Team:
4D Team

Design Firm:
Incubis Consultants (India) Pvt. Ltd

Project:
Design of Food & Beverage Kiosks for MIAL T2

Client:
Lite Bite Travel Foods

Design Team:
S. Paldas, Silky Arora, Piyush Chandra, Ajay Anand, Ayush Jain, Gunveen Kaur, Palak Mittal, Mohd. Naushad, Mohd. Usman, Adeeba Kazmi, Amandeep Kaur, Amit Krishn Gulati

ABOUT THE PROJECT

Incubis created 10 iconic food and beverage kiosks for the spectacular new T2 terminal at Mumbai in close coordination with the client and the airport developer, the GVK group, to ensure that each kiosk and its adjacent customer area become unique focal points within the passenger spaces.

KEY FEATURES

- Innovative use of materials & processes to achieve complex geometries
- Bespoke, modular and pre-engineered for rapid assembly on site
- Nashto — Inspired by traditional Indian utensil forms & textures
- Baker Street — A folded twist on nautical maps
- Zambar — Kerala saree motifs wrapped around a glass 'gopuram' with the show kitchen
- Street foods of India — A double-decker bus!

259 Okhla Industrial Estate, Phase III,
New Delhi 110 020, Delhi

Mr Amit Krishn Gulati

+91 98101 17072, +91 11 4311 0500
+91 11 4311 0510

incubis@incubis.net

www.incubis.net

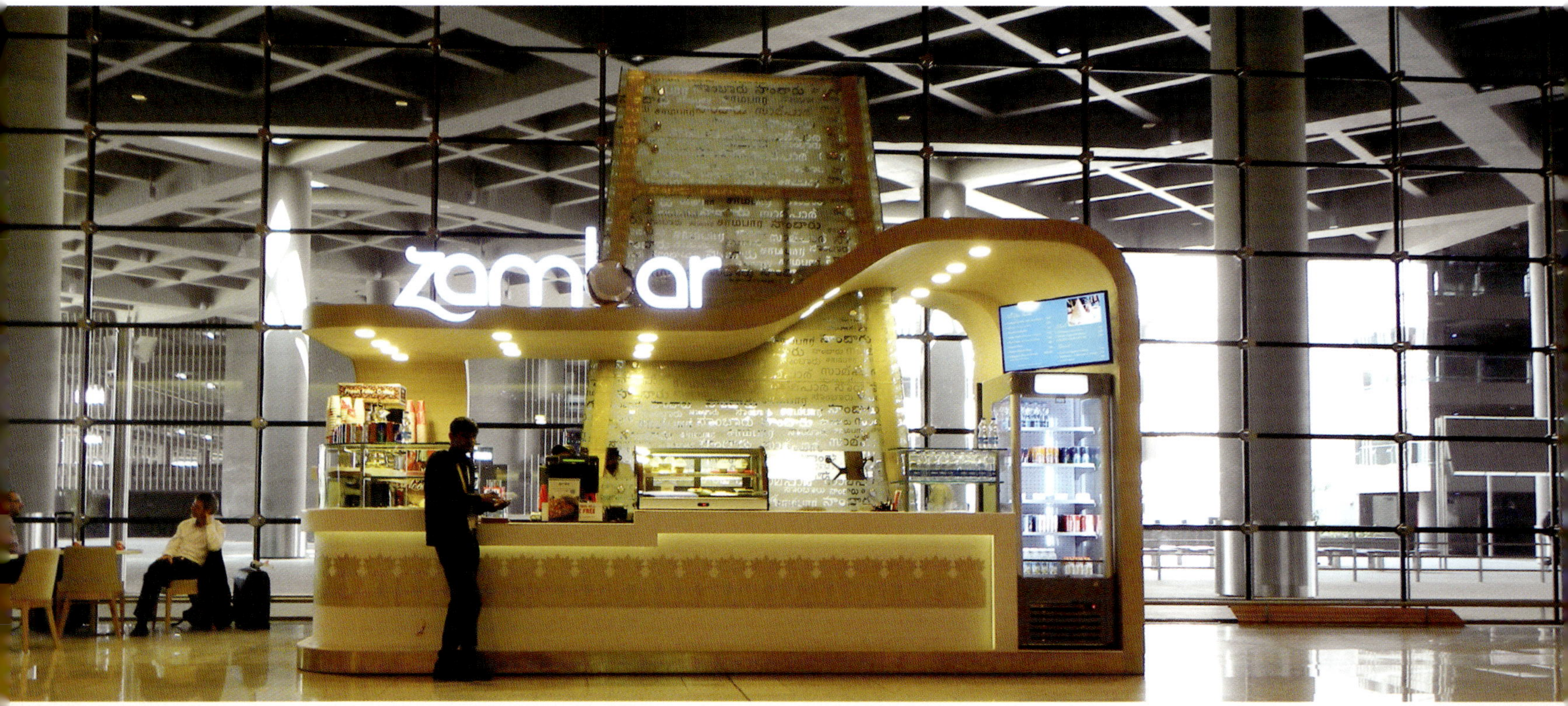

LOPEZ DESIGN

ABOUT THE PROJECT

At Mercer Noida, Lopez Design seamlessly merged storytelling, graphics and interior design to create a compelling and dynamic workspace. The designers envisaged a contemporary environment in varied themes and colours that reflected the philosophy of the firm encouraging vibrant involvement. Mercer's diverse culture, global expanse and connectivity were expressed through a passionate exploration of materials and media.

Design Firm:
Lopez Design

Project:
Mercer Noida Facility

Client:
Mercer Consulting (India) Pvt. Ltd

Design Team:
Anthony Lopez, Joanna Mendes, Ashish Rehani, Aparajita Ninan, Jonak Das, Divya Verma, Shruti Shyam, Deeksha Kumar

EXCELLENCE AWARDS 014

KEY FEATURES

- Branding through space design
- Immersive environmental graphics
- Visual storytelling in space
- Company ethos reflected in environment
- Thematic break-out areas
- Transformation of the corporate environment to a warm, energetic space
- Revival of etched and stained glass
- Exploration of custom designs in veneer & vinyl

145/1B, Shahpur Jat Village,
New Delhi 110 049

Anthony Lopez

+91 11 2649 9004 / 05 / 06

info@lopezdesign.com

www.lopezdesign.com

ABOUT THE PROJECT

This coffee-table book commemorates the silver jubilee of Microland while tracing its evolution and growth over the past 25 years. Divided into sections that mark each phase of this journey, the book is part-history, part-memoir. Peppered with anecdotes and incidents, it is an interesting look back at the 25 years that have made Microland the company it is today.

Design Firm:
Rivet Design Studio

Project:
Shaping the Future: The Microland Story

Client:
Microland Ltd

Design Team:
Team Rivet

KEY FEATURES

- 182-page book tracing the 25-year history of Microland, from start-up to hybrid IT pioneer
- Divided into 4 phases, correlated with developments in IT
- Showcases photographs, newspaper clippings and advertisements from the time period
- Features contributions from Microland leaders and customers

1197/1, 3rd Cross, HAL 3rd Stage,
New Thippasandra Post,
Bangalore 560 075, Karnataka

Ms Amee Nagraj, Mr Sandeep K.R.

+91 98455 57521, +91 99001 61029

amee@rivetdesign.in
sandeep@rivetdesign.in

www.rivetdesign.in

ABOUT THE PROJECT

Paperboat drinks are all about reliving timeless childhood memories with every flavour. The gift pack is an extension of this brand philosophy. It is inspired by an old trunk, an icon of memories and cherished objects that one has preserved from their past — trophies, albums, toys and keepsakes. This appealed to us as the perfect packaging format to hold these precious life objects for many years to come.

KEY FEATURES

- Simple
- Minimalistic
- Quirky
- Reusable

Lakeview Farm, Near Shell Petrol Pump,
Whitefield — Old Airport Road,
Ramagondanahalli, Bangalore 560 066,
Karnataka

Shipra Bhargava

+91 88842 11132, +91 80285 43061

shipra@studioabd.in

www.studioabd.in

Design Firm:
Studio ABD Design Services Pvt. Ltd

Project:
Paperboat Drinks Festive Gift Pack

Client:
Hector Beverages Pvt. Ltd

Design Team:
Abhijit Bansod, Ajith Jose

ACKNOWLEDGEMENTS

The Confederation of Indian Industry (CII) would like to thank Mr Udayant Malhoutra, Chairman, CII National Committee on Design, and Mr Navroze Godrej, Co-Chairman, and the members of the CII National Committee on Design for their encouragement and guidance in bringing about this landmark publication on contemporary Indian design. We also place on record our thanks to Mr Dipendra Baoni and his team at Lemon Design for putting the entire book together, and to Penguin Books for publishing the book.

We express our sincere appreciation to the Editorial Board of this publication for reviewing the entries received. We thank the design agencies and industry members for contributing their excellent work with us, which truly make this book a collector's item.

Design Partner

Lemon Design Pvt. Ltd, Pune

Creative Director
Dipendra Singh Baoni

Design Team
Manosij Sarkar, Reshma Mallecha and Mihir Bankapure

INDUSTRIAL DESIGN

INTERACTION DESIGN

MOBILITY DESIGN

VISUAL COMMUNICATION

THE CII DESIGN YEARBOOK 2014 CONTAINS THE BEST ENTRIES IN DESIGN FOR THE YEAR 2013–14. THE DESIGN YEARBOOK IS A MEDIUM TO COMMUNICATE THE BEST OF DESIGN EMANATING FROM THOSE COUNTRIES IN DIVERSE DESIGN DISCIPLINES. THESE YEARBOOKS BECOME AN INTERNATIONAL REFERENCE FOR EXCELLENT DESIGN. COMPANIES, JOURNALISTS, ARCHITECTS, PLANNERS, DESIGNERS AND PEOPLE ALL OVER THE WORLD WHO ARE INTERESTED IN DESIGN USE THE YEARBOOKS FOR THEIR DAY-TO-DAY WORK AND KEEP THEM OVER THE YEARS AS A COLLECTOR'S ITEM AND AN ARCHIVE OF EXCELLENT DESIGN.

THE CII DESIGN YEARBOOK — THE FIRST SUCH ENDEAVOUR FROM INDIA AIMS TO CAPTURE OVER 200 RECENT PROJECTS IN WHICH THE COMPANIES / DESIGN FIRMS HAVE EMPLOYED AGILE DESIGN THINKING, METHODOLOGIES AND PROCESSES TO ACHIEVE SUCCESS FOR CLIENTS, PARTNERS AND END USERS.

COMBINING AN EXPERIENCED EDITORIAL TEAM AND AN INNOVATIVE GRAPHIC DESIGN, THE YEARBOOK WILL BE A COMPILATION OF EXCEPTIONAL DESIGN IN INDIA. A WIDE RANGE OF PROJECTS WILL BE PRESENTED IN THE VOLUME FROM 4 DIFFERENT CATEGORIES VIZ. VISUAL COMMUNICATION, INDUSTRIAL DESIGN, INTERACTION DESIGN AND MOBILITY DESIGN. EACH PROJECT IS PRESENTED WITH A SELECTION OF IMAGES AND ACCOMPANYING TEXT.